A Lasting Peace

A Lasting Peace

CAROL LYNN PEARSON

International Standard Book Number:
0-934126-38-0
First Printing September 1983

Randall Book
9500 South 500 West, Suite 103
Salt Lake City, Utah 84070

This story is based on a number of historical incidents that have been reported as true.

CHAPTER ONE

S ol did not always hurry through breakfast so he could get the chores done. But this morning he did. He picked up the bowl and drank the last of the cornmeal mush and milk instead of using his spoon like a civilized person. His mother would get after him for that, but she wasn't in the kitchen. She had eaten earlier with his father and was out milking the cows. Grandma was the only one at the table with him, and she hardly got after Sol for anything.

"You're coming today, aren't you, Grandma?" Sol asked, putting down his bowl.

"Certainly I am," said Grandma. "Wouldn't miss a party for anything!"

"Better hurry up, then," said Sol, as he pushed his chair back and took his bowl over to the dishpan.

"I'll hurry." Grandma smiled, winked at him, and then picked up her bowl and drank the last of the cornmeal mush and milk.

"Party" wasn't really the right word. "Celebration" was. Every year since they had arrived in the Utah territory six years ago in 1851, Sol looked forward to the Fourth of July for months and months. A frontier celebration was not like anything they had known back East. Wrestling matches—lots of food—music and dancing—trading.

Sol especially liked to watch the trading. The Indians always brought their horses, furs, buckskins, baskets, and blankets to trade to the White settlers for sacks of grain, potatoes, dried corn, dried peaches, and anything else the White man had that an Indian might take a fancy to.

Sol's father, John McAllister, wanted a lasting peace with the Indians, and so he would probably spend his time talking with Arrowpine, chief of the Utes, developing their friendship.

But more than anything else in the world Sol wanted a horse of his own, and so he would be watching the trading, dreaming of the day when he would find the horse he was looking for. He would know her when he saw her.

Sol ran into the barn and saw his mother seated on a stool by Daisy's large bag, squirting milk into the bucket.

"Can I milk?" asked Sol. He'd much rather milk than feed the pigs.

Sol's father emerged from behind another cow and said, "Sure, son. I'll get the wagon ready. Finish off Matilda here and meet me out front."

"I'll be right there, Pa. I milk as good as a man."

John heard his wife laugh and turned to her. "Well, you do too, Paula. You milk as good as a man!"

With a quick twist of her wrist, Paula shot a stream of foaming milk directly into her husband's eye. "If I didn't have to wash your clothes, I'd dump this whole bucket on you! As good as a man! I'll have you know, John McAllister, that I can not only get milk into the bucket as quick as any man, but this cow and I can *make* it. And that's something no man alive can *ever* do!"

John laughed and wiped his face with the sleeve of his red shirt. Sol liked to hear his parents joking and laughing. It was like a weather vane that told him the winds were blowing in a good direction.

Sol milked hard, trying to keep up with his mother's steady rhythm. He had good long fingers like hers, and he had her clear blue eyes. His sandy hair and square jaw were inherited from his father. He was twelve years old now and tall. Just last month the book that he and his mother put on their heads as they stood backs together had tipped in his mother's direction. "Pa," Sol had gone out yelling. "I'm taller. I'm taller than Ma!"

Sol walked as fast as he could with a bucket of milk in each hand and took them into the kitchen. Now to get that wagon loaded with the kegs of molasses they were taking along for trading.

"You bringing that horse?" Sol stopped in amazement as he watched his father lead Balky from the barn.

"Yep. I've been working with him, and it's about time he learned who's boss."

Balky was a large brown horse that was named after his chief characteristic, the way animals named "Speedy" or "Spot" or "Ragtail" were named after theirs. Balky was stubborn. If he didn't want to move, he didn't move. He would balk whenever he chose, which was most of the time. Balky was definitely not the horse of Sol's dreams.

"Come on, Balky, come on." John's voice was soothing and firm as he hitched the horse to the wagon. Then he jumped up onto the wooden seat and took the reins, shaking them lightly and clicking his tongue. "Giddiup."

The horse did not move. John shook the reins harder, slapping leather across the animal's back. "Giddiup!" he said sharply. Balky did not move.

Sol watched his father's face harden. John did not use cuss words. Good Mormons did not swear at all, and John McAllister was a good Mormon. But Sol figured that his father was thinking some pretty good cuss words about now.

"Move, dang you anyway!" John laid the reins as hard as he could on the horse's back. Balky shuddered a little like he did when a fly landed. But his feet did not move.

John jumped down from the wagon. "Climb on up there,

son," he said.

Sol quickly got up on the wagon and took the reins.

"Now, once we get moving, don't let him stop. Don't stop for anything. You understand?"

"Yes, Pa."

John put a hand on the horse's halter and nudged him forward. "Come on, Balky. Come on."

The horse whinnied and planted himself deeper into the barnyard soil.

John jerked harder. "Come on, you no-good, slab-sided excuse for a horse. Move!" He jerked the halter again. Reluctantly Balky began to move. John walked beside him, still pulling the halter. "Don't let him stop," he called back to Sol. "No matter what!"

"But what about the molasses? And Grandma?"

"You just circle the house. I'll get them on."

"Pa?"

"Yes?"

"Why don't we just take another horse?"

"'Cause this one has to learn sometime. And today's the day."

"Oh."

John walked to the porch of the log house, the horse and Sol behind him. He picked up a thirty-pound keg of molasses and as the horse and the boy passed by, he slung it up onto the wagon.

"That's it, son. Just keep moving."

Sol guided the horse around the back of the house. Grandma peered out the bedroom window, and he waved at her. She smiled and waved back. Again the wagon approached the little porch, and again a thirty-pound keg of molasses was slung up beside the first. Again Sol circled the house, and again Grandma peered out of the bedroom window. Sol smiled again and waved. Grandma smiled and waved back.

After the eighth trip around the house, Grandma appeared on the porch, followed by Sol's mother.

"Have you young fools lost all the sense the good Lord gave you?" asked Grandma, leaning on her cane and staring out through pale blue eyes. Grandma was pastel. She seemed all blues and pinks and grays to look at. Which was what threw a lot of people off, because her personality was not pastel at all, and once in a while she even spoke in scarlet.

"Never you mind, Grandma," said John. "We're just loading up this balky horse, and we can't have him stop for nothing. You just line up with the molasses. It'll be your turn in a minute. You jump on when I do, Paula. You jump as good as a man."

Grandma chuckled. Then she laughed, the sound wheezing its way out of her rib cage and up through her throat. With the aid of her cane she obediently went to the end of the line and stood chortling beside a keg of molasses. Each time John slung a keg up onto the wagon, Grandma clapped her hands and chuckled anew as if she had just been told a good joke.

"Here they come, Grandma. Your turn!"

"John—be careful." Paula took a hesitant step toward them.

Sol and the wagon came around the house. Grandma wheezed and chuckled and held out her arms to her son. John McAllister picked his mother up as easily as if she were a thirty-pound keg of molasses and deftly placed her on the wagon seat beside Sol. Grandma whooped in delight and clapped her hands.

"Climb on, Paula!" John ran around to the other side of the moving wagon and jumped up on the wagon bed, sitting down beside his son. Paula lifted her skirts and climbed on the other side. The wagon jostled with the sudden addition of weight. And the horse stopped.

"Oh, no," moaned Sol, putting his head in his hands.

Grandma was laughing so hard she could barely breathe. She put her hands over her mouth like a naughty child who has got the giggles during prayer.

John sighed and shook his head. Then he lifted the reins and slapped them over Balky's back. "Come on. Giddiap. Giddiap!"

The horse lowered his head and nibbled at a small patch of grass.

John stood up and slapped the reins again as hard as he could. Sol knew his father would not whip Balky. He had never seen him whip an animal in his life. And plenty of animals had given him cause.

The veins stood out in John's neck as he continued to slap the horse. "Move, confound it! Move, you son of perdition!"

Son of perdition? Sol had never heard his father call anything that. It wasn't really a cuss word, but it was about the lowest thing anybody could come to in Mormon belief. It was worse even than just plain going to hell. John must be pretty angry.

"Move!" John continued to shout at the creature. "Move, or may you burn in ---." John stopped before he said the bad word, but evidently he had gotten an idea. Quickly he jumped down from the wagon, disappeared into the shed by the side of the house, and in a moment came out with a handful of kindling and a couple of small logs.

He knelt down beside the horse and directly under the animal's belly arranged the kindling.

Paula gasped. "John . . ."

"We all need a little motivation," said John.

Flint hit steel, and in a moment wisps of smoke curled upward from the little pile of kindling. John climbed onto the wagon, took the reins in hand, and waited. Balky continued to browse for grass, his feet still planted firmly. As the first effect of the fire was felt, he flicked his tail toward his belly, as if to shoo away a fly. His hide shuddered, and he flicked again. Then he snorted and swayed from side to side, still without moving forward. All eyes were fastened on the flames that leaped higher and higher. In a moment they licked the belly of the horse. Balky whinnied and reared back. Then he moved. A quick trot took him about ten feet forward — where he stopped, with the flames directly under the wagon.

John sputtered and jumped to his feet. "Giddiap!" he shouted.

Grandma wheezed out a giant laugh and slapped her hands on her leg again and again.

Sol and Paula both looked at John. John slapped the reins hard against the horse's back. "Move, you . . . you miserable animal. Move, you . . ."

With a quick motion, Grandma grabbed the reins and stood up, snapping the reins with the sound of a shotgun. "Damn you to hell," she shrieked. "Now, you get a-moving!"

The horse lurched forward and began to trot down the road. Grandma handed the reins back to John and smiled. "You forget, son, that this here horse is not a Mormon. You got to speak to him like he understands. And *I* get to talk to him that way because *I'm* not a Mormon either!"

Sol sucked in his cheeks, trying to keep a straight face. Grandma wheezed into a new spell of laughter. John shook his head and smiled. And the horse continued down the road at a fast trot.

It was true that Grandma was not a Mormon. When her only son and his wife joined the Mormon Church back in South Carolina and moved to Illinois, she agreed to go with them, but she was not about to exchange her deeply-held Presbyterianism for any new-fangled religion. She crossed the plains with them to come to Utah only because life with no family would be worse than life in a Western desert. And by and large it had worked out fine.

Sol loved Grandma. As a small boy he had loved to climb into her bed on cold winter mornings. Her bed had always smelled of lavendar, and it was always warm. She had told him stories about life back home on their cotton plantation. And the wonderful parties. And the horses.

And now that he was big he loved to sit with her out on the porch in the evenings and philosophize about life. Just last night they had had a conversation that Sol would remember for a long time.

"Sol," Grandma had said, pulling her light blue shawl up around her thin shoulders. "Do you want to know the secret to everybody in the world living happily together? Do you?"

"Sure, Grandma." Sol scooted in closer to her. That sounded like a secret that would be good to know.

"Are you ready?"

Sol nodded.

"'Do unto others,'" Grandma spoke quietly and mysteriously. "'As you would have others do unto you.'"

Sol scowled at her. "Aw, Grandma. That's no secret. I've heard the Golden Rule a hundred times."

"Well, sure," Grandma smiled. "Almost everybody's heard it in one way or another. But do you know what they *don't* know?"

Sol leaned in and shook his head.

Grandma pursed her lips and nodded her head for a moment. Then she narrowed her eyes, looked directly into Sol's and spoke in a whisper. "It works!" She smiled and lifted her face to the moonlight.

Sol sat on the log fence in the shade of a large tree watching the horse trading. Horses of all colors and sizes were there with Indian or white man—spotted Appaloosas—ponies that were full-grown but small—black, brown, white, gray horses—a few palominos, beautiful and golden.

Suddenly Sol's eyes fell on a black filly that was being led toward him by a short, fat Indian who shuffled along in the dust in contrast to the clear, precise dance of the filly as she followed obediently.

Sol raised himself a little to see better. His stomach pushed closer to his heart, and his jaw dropped as he watched the young horse come nearer. He had drawn pictures of this animal, talked about her, dreamed about her. Dozens of pictures were nailed into the logs of a wall of his room, identical in every way to the filly he was looking at, down to the five-point star on her black forehead and the white boots on three of her black legs. His mother had corrected his first drawings and changed the star to a diamond because no horses have real stars. But Sol changed it back again because his horse did.

He jumped off the fence and ran to where the Indian was tying up Star with the other horses. Sol knew her name was Star, and he knew she was about a year old. He had wanted a filly, one young enough for him to grow up with. Not that he wasn't pretty much grown up already.

"Hey, hey!" said a man admiringly, putting out a hand to touch the shiny neck of the filly. "Not too bad for an Injun nag. What do you want for her?"

Sol had never seen this man before and already he disliked him. It wasn't the large belly that hung out over his thick leather belt, or the pock marks that completely covered his face except for where the heavy brown mustache was. It was the eyes that drew themselves into little slits when he spoke, sort of like windows closing to keep something hidden.

"What you have?" asked the Indian, laying out on the ground the stack of blankets he was carrying.

"Wheat. Two bushel for that there filly."

An older Indian muttered something in Ute and moved his hands in a disgusted gesture.

"More." The Indian opened Star's mouth to show off her perfect teeth. "Good horse. Need more."

The white man's eyes narrowed further. You can tell more by a man's eyes than a horse's mouth, Sol thought to himself, concluding that he wouldn't trust this man as far as he could throw him.

The man smiled and pulled a jack-knife out of his pocket. Slowly, as if he were working a miracle, he made two blades appear. The Indian's face lit up, and he reached for the shiny knife, opening and closing the blades.

"Some knife, huh? Betcha never seen no knife like that before, huh, Injun?"

In Ute the Indian spoke rapidly to the other red man. The old Indian gestured disdainfully and pushed the jack-knife away.

"The knife and two bushels of wheat for that there horse. Deal?"

Sol watched wide-eyed. A horse like Star was worth far more than a couple of bushels of wheat and a jack-knife. Why, that jack-knife was no better than the one in his own pocket, and he had got his for fifty cents. But if you'd never seen one before—maybe. . .

Eagerly the Indian nodded his head. "Good."

"On second thought . . ." The man's eyes narrowed again. "This here knife is such a prize that I'm not sure I want to part with it. How about two, three blankets along with the horse?"

More? He was asking for more?

The old Indian shrieked and said something in Ute. Then he grabbed the knife and threw it at the white man's feet. But the short, fat Indian lunged for it and wiped the dust off the blades with his loin cloth.

With practiced poise, the white man reached for the knife. "Too much? Then I'll just take my knife back. You don't see a knife like that very often, I tell you."

The Indian stepped back, holding the knife close. "No. Want knife. Horse and three blankets."

"Well, I don't know," drawled the white man. "That is some knife you got there."

"Four blankets," said the Indian.

"Deal," said the white man.

The old Indian shrieked again, turned and walked away.

Sol watched in fascination as the exchange was made, and the white man put his rope around Star and led her to his wagon. A mixture of admiration and contempt filled him. The man had not dealt fairly with the Indian, that was clear. But he had got what he wanted. More than he wanted, really. Good thing Sol's father hadn't been there. He would have done something about it. He believed in being absolutely fair and honest with the Indians. Sol agreed with his father. Still, the man with the slit eyes had got what he wanted.

"Who is that man?" Sol asked his father as they sat together to watch the wrestling matches. The large pock-marked man was leaning against a tree, chewing tobacco and spitting every now and then as if something he hated were on the ground in front of him.

"Haven't met him," replied his father. "But he was pointed out to me. Nat Kohler's his name. He's our new neighbor. Bought the place just south of ours."

Their neighbor? Star would be in a pasture nearby? Maybe he could go see her every once in a while.

"We'll have to go on over and welcome him. It's important to get along with your neighbors."

"Yeah," said Sol. But he didn't really think his father was going to get along with this one. John McAllister was patient with dumb animals. But not with stupid human beings. Or dishonest ones. Or cruel ones. Sol had inherited not only his father's thick, sandy hair, but his ethics as well. So he felt pretty much the same way. But Sol had noticed by this time in his life that being nice doesn't always pay off. At least right away. And he found himself staring in fascination at Nat Kohler, leaning against the tree and spitting.

"Who's first?" called out Jenkins Broadhead, standing in the center of a hand-marked ring and grinning widely. The wrestling matches were a favorite of the men who came to the frontier celebrations, and the winner was traditionally given as much ice cream and pie as he could eat.

"I am!" Nat Kohler jumped into the ring, unbuttoning his shirt and revealing a mass of black hair on a thick, barrel chest.

"And who will challenge the newcomer?" asked Jenkins. "Let's show him the kind of men he's moved in with."

The men on the rough wooden benches looked at one another. "Go to it, Hal," said one. "You can take him easy!"

The others laughed as the man who had spoken pushed a skinny fellow toward the ring.

"Yourself!" said the skinny man, darting back to his seat.

"I'll take you all, one at a time," bellowed Nat Kohler, flexing his muscles and looking at the crowd through the little slits of his eyes. "But I want me a Injun first!"

A quick leap landed him directly in front of an Indian brave who leapt to his feet as if threatened by a mountain lion. Then the men stared at each other for a moment in silence. The the Indian nodded his head and cautiously, arms out like a tight rope walker, made his way past Kohler into the center of the ring.

Kohler laughed and stripped off his shirt, throwing it back toward the tree. It caught in a low branch and swung there like a red flag.

"You going to keep all them clothes on, Injun?" he taunted the red man who wore only a loin cloth and moccasins.

Some of the white men laughed. And some looked uncomfortably at each other and at John McAllister.

"What's he up to?" John said quietly to his son. "You don't make fun of the Indians when you have to live in the same valley with them."

The two men in the ring circled one another. Then Kohler lunged for the Indian's middle, but the Indian dropped to the earth, and Kohler tripped on him, falling headlong onto the ground. White men and red men both cheered, and Kohler angrily began to get up. But the Indian quickly sprang on top of him and forced his torso to the ground. Jenkins began to count. "One . . . two . . ." Whoever could hold the other down for the count of five was the winner. "Three . . ."

Suddenly Kohler's open hand smashed into the Indian's face, and the red man yelped in pain. John jumped to his feet.

"No hitting!" he cried.

A few Indians jumped up, shouting in their own language. Blood was dripping from the Indian's nose as Kohler turned over and pinned the red man beneath him.

"Don't count!" yelled John. "The rules are no hitting!"

"Count, damn you!" panted Kohler.

Confused, Jenkins began the count, then stopped.

"Count!" yelled Kohler.

The Indian struggled beneath him. Chief Arrowpine and another brave leapt to their feet, heading for the ring. In an instant John was beside them, his hands on their shoulders.

"No, Chief," he said. "Let them be."

"One . . . two . . ." Kohler was counting for himself. "Three . . . four . . . five!" Triumphantly Kohler jumped up from the ground and raised his hands above his head. The Indian put both hands to his nose and stumbled back to his place.

"Who's next?" shouted Kohler. "Any more Injuns want to have a try?" Then he pointed at Arrowpine. "How about you, Chief? Come on . . . I always wanted to wrestle me a real Injun chief."

Trembling with rage, Arrowpine walked into the ring and shook his fist in Kohler's face. "No wrestle with you! *No* Indian wrestle with you. You wrestle dirty. No fight fair!"

"Aw, come on, Chief, You afraid to fight a white man, huh?"

"No afraid!" shouted Arrowpine.

"Then choose your man. Choose any white man here. Come on, Chief!"

"I not trust white man. All white man cheat Indian. Only one white man I trust. I wrestle . . ." And here the chief turned to the white man at his side. ". . . John Mac."

After a moment's silence, the Indians began to hoot enthusiastically. Then the white men began to cheer. Sol looked at his father being pushed toward the ring by his friends. His father was not a wrestler. He was a brave man, but not unusually strong, and had no taste for physical violence. He wanted peace—peace for all people, but especially for the whites and the Indians. And here he was invited to wrestle by the chief of the Utes, and if he refused, the chief would not like it much.

"Go get him, John!" yelled a white man.

"Scalp him!" cried another.

John put out his hand to Arrowpine, and Arrowpine took it. The two men shook hands solemnly. Sol was glad his mother was over with Grandma making ice cream. She would not like this.

The wrestling match took approximately five minutes. John hadn't wrestled a grown man before, but he'd thrown plenty of steers, so he tried to adapt. Once he had the chief on the ground and Jenkins began to count, but before he reached three Arrowpine was on his feet with a blood-curdling shriek and with lightning speed threw John over his shoulders and onto his back. The force of the chief landing on him took his breath away.

Sol jumped to his feet as he saw the chief draw from his belt a glittering knife and hold it in scalping position above his father's head. Quickly Arrowpine performed a mock scalping as Jenkins counted. "One . . . two . . . three . . . four . . . five!" Whoops of triumph went up from the Indians, and Sol sat down again, shaking.

Arrowpine helped John to his feet, smiling broadly. John smiled back and held out his hand.

"Congratulations, Chief," he said.

Arrowpine brushed aside John's hand and put his arms around him in a tight embrace. The two men slapped each other's backs for a moment, then broke apart.

As John and Sol left the wrestling area, John put an arm around Sol's shoulders and said, "Well, we won."

"We did?" asked Sol.

"If the Indians had left on the warpath, we might have seen some trouble in a few days or a few weeks. You got to keep your eye on the bigger picture, son. Arrowpine won. And so did we."

Sol's father was good at keeping his eye on the bigger picture. And Sol could never quite figure out how he did it.

CHAPTER TWO

It was nearly sunset and time to leave the celebration. Sol wandered a little ways toward the creek, where he knew Kohler's wagon was. And Star. He sat down about fifty feet away, with his back against a tree stump and stared. It had not been a dream. There she was. And Kohler had got her for two bushels of wheat and a jack-knife! Sol reached into his pocket and pulled out his knife. He opened the blade and flipped it toward the ground. The blade buried itself in the brown earth, and the white handle shone in the sun. Sol liked to see how many times in a row he could put the knife in the ground. Once he had done it fifty-eight times straight. He pulled the knife out, wiped it off, and pushed the blade back into the handle.

"Knife have elbow."

Sol turned to see Chief Arrowpine standing behind him. The chief looked even taller than Sol remembered. Or maybe it was just that Sol was sitting on the ground. And the sun behind his feathered headdress made sort of a halo, like Sol had seen in religious paintings before they moved out West.

Sol held out the knife for the chief to look at. "The blades go in and out of the handle. See?" He pushed the two blades in and out to demonstrate.

A smile broke over the brown, wrinkled face, and the chief hunched down beside Sol, taking the knife into his hands and moving the blades in and out. "Smart knife. Very smart knife," he said.

Sol stared at the chief. Down on his level, he didn't look so big—just like everybody else.

"You trade knife to Arrowpine. What you want?"

Trade? Sol didn't want to give up his knife. But how do you say no to the chief of the Utes? Besides, he could easily get another one.

"What do you have?"

"Blankets. Knife worth—one Indian blanket."

Sol thought a moment. "Five blankets," he said.

The chief's eyes narrowed, and he looked at Sol. "You John Mac son?"

"Yes."

Arrowpine nodded slowly. "Good. Five blankets."

Sol looked down at the knife. Five blankets? That easy? Were all Indians as gullible as the one that had traded Star? Even the chief?

"Well, I don't know, now that I think about it," said Sol. "I'm pretty attached to this knife. You don't see one like it every day."

The chief studied his face carefully. "You want . . . more?"

"How about that elk-tooth necklace?"

The chief was wearing around his neck nine large elk teeth with lumps of polished black stones between strung on a piece of rawhide. His brown fingers went to his neck. "Necklace, too?" he asked evenly.

Sol nodded. Arrowpine slowly took off the necklace and handed it to Sol. Sol held out the jack-knife and put it in the chief's hand.

* * * * * * * * * *

John McAllister looked at his son in disbelief. "You traded what?"

Sol climbed into the wagon and placed the five Indian blankets on the seat beside him. His mother stopped arranging the dishes in the basket and looked from her son to her husband.

"I traded my knife to Arrowpine. He must have wanted it real bad—gave me five blankets plus . . ." He held it up proudly. "This necklace."

"Son." John pulled his legs over the wagon bench so he was facing Sol directly. "That knife was worth about one blanket. You cheated Arrowpine."

"But *he* didn't know that. He was happy with the trade."

"But I know you cheated him, son." John leaned in and forced Sol to look him in the eyes. "And you know you cheated him."

"But everybody else does. The Indians *expect* it."

"And that's why they don't trust the white man. How can they trust us when we cheat them every time we get the chance?"

Sol felt his cheeks become hot. He had hurt his father, and he hated it. "But . . . but . . ." he concluded weakly. "Everybody else does it."

John put a hand on his son's knee and said softly and simply, "I don't care what everybody else does. As for me and my house . . . we deal honestly with the Indians. I have never lied to an Indian, and I have never cheated one. And I'm not going to, and neither are you. You go find Arrowpine. And you come back with *one* blanket."

"Find him? He's probably left already," protested Sol.

"We'll wait right here for you. I don't care if you have to follow him all the way to the Ute encampment. Don't come back until you've made things right with Arrowpine."

Helplessly, Sol looked at his mother, who smiled and nodded. Then John, Paula, and Grandma climbed off the wagon.

Sol was right. Arrowpine had already gone. Sol scoured the area and then set off in the direction of the Ute encampment. Good thing it was not very far away. How humiliating — to have to face the chief and apologize for cheating him. Why couldn't Sol's father be like everybody else's father?

Sol pulled slightly on the reins as he spotted some figures up ahead. They looked like Indians. He would ask them how far ahead Arrowpine was. Coming closer, Sol saw that four Indians were seated by the side of the road with their horses hitched to the fence. Seeing him, one of the Indians stood up. It was . . . Could it be? Arrowpine?

Sol stopped his horse directly in front of the chief, a squaw, and two braves.

"Arrowpine? I . . . I was coming to find you."

"I know."

"You know?"

"I wait here. I know you come back."

Sol stared at him in amazement. "How did you know that?"

The chief folded his arms across his chest and looked at Sol. "You John Mac son. John Mac honest with Indian. Always. Make son be honest, too. I know you come back."

Sol took four Indian blankets from the wagon seat beside him and handed them to the chief. Then he took from around his neck the elk-tooth necklace and reluctantly placed it in Arrowpine's outstretched hand.

With no further words, the Indians untied their horses, mounted them, and rode off. Sol watched until they disappeared over a small hill. Then he turned the wagon around and rode in the opposite direction.

They drove toward home silently. Grandma leaned back and dozed, and Paula rolled up her shawl and put it under Grandma's neck to make her more comfortable.

"I think we'll just stop in here at Nat Kohler's for a few

minutes before we go home," said John, as he turned the wagon toward the new neighbor's yard. "Got one keg of molasses left over. How about we give it to the Kohlers as a little present to welcome them to the neighborhood?"

"Sounds like a good, friendly idea," said Paula.

As they drove up to Kohler's place, a large log house with several barns and chicken coops and a big brown dog panting beside a small tree, Sol turned to his father.

"What if Mr. Kohler doesn't feel like being friendly?"

"Well, I do," replied John. "And I don't let other people decide how I want to behave."

But Mr. Kohler was friendly. He came out of the house at the sound of the dog's barking and greeted them warmly, shaking hands with both John and Sol and giving a nod to Grandma and Paula.

"Brought you some molasses," said John, swinging down the keg.

"Well, thank you. Thank you a lot."

Nat Kohler was as large as Sol remembered him. And there were as many pock marks on his face as Sol remembered, too. And his eyes peered out from their narrow slits as if through half-open windows. Sol studied him quietly as Kohler and his father talked. Then his eyes moved to the barn. Was Star in there? Could he maybe see her?

"All the sugar we brought with us from the East went pretty fast," said John. "A few years ago the brethren brought over from France machinery that filled forty heavy wagons for a sugar beet factory and five hundred bushel of seeds. But the soil in Utah changed the chemical makeup of the beets. Anyway, 'bout the best we can do just now is this here molasses from sugar cane."

"Well, the missus will be right pleased with that."

Sol looked around for some sign of Mr. Kohler's family. A thin gray-headed woman was peering out from a window, but drew back as if not wanting to be seen. And two small, ragged girls giggled and pushed each other out from behind the chicken coop.

"Uh . . . Mr. Kohler?" Sol spoke quickly before his courage failed him.

"Yeah?"

"That filly . . . the one you got today from the Indian . . . is she . . . here?"

Kohler laughed. "Shore she's here. You got some business with her?"

Sol blushed and looked down at the ground, kicking a little rock toward the wagon wheel. "I sort of wondered if . . . if I could see her."

"You like that filly, huh?"

"Yeah."

"Don't see why not."

The big man lumbered toward the barn, and Sol followed.

"You want to get down, Grandma?" asked John.

"Nope. I'm too busy," replied Grandma, leaning back and closing her eyes. "You go along."

Paula stayed with Grandma, and Sol and John followed Nat Kohler into the barn. Everybody's barn smells alike, thought Sol — leather and hay. He liked the smell of a barn.

And there she was, right there in the first stall. Star. She was just as beautiful as Sol remembered. And the white star on her forehead looked like a generous snowflake had alighted and decided not to melt. She really was beautiful.

"You like that filly, huh?" Kohler smiled as he said it, as if there were something amusing in the idea.

Sol almost said, "I *love* her," but he wasn't sure Kohler understood very much about love, and he didn't want to be laughed at. So Sol just nodded his head.

"Can I . . . can I touch her?"

"Sure."

Reverently Sol approached the stall and put out his hand. The filly whinnied and took a step toward him, sticking her head out of the stall. With one finger he touched the white star, gently tracing its five points. Then he stroked her nose and her neck. A smile broke over his face, and he put his cheek up next to hers. "Hi, Star," he said quietly. "Hi, Star."

"He likes the filly," said Kohler, gesturing toward Sol with a long piece of straw he held between his teeth.

"Yep," said John.

Kohler grabbed a long-toothed metal comb from a hook and tossed it to Sol. "Just as well make yourself useful. You want to curry her?"

"Yeah!" Sol's eyes lit up like a child entering the room on Christmas morning. He climbed in the stall and ran the comb over her black hide, talking softly to her.

"He likes the filly," Kohler said again. "Hey, boy! You can come brush and curry her any time you want. And feed her. Long as you throw a little food to the rest of the horses. And clean her stall once in a while."

"I can?" Sol knew that Kohler was looking for free labor, but that didn't matter. If he could just be with Star—he'd do anything. "Did you hear that, Star? I can come take care of you."

"Star?"

"That's her name."

Kohler chuckled. "Her name's Star."

John sat down on a bale of hay and folded his arms. "Anything I can help you with? Or tell you about the area?"

"Nope." Kohler sat down on another bale and arranged a wad of chewing tobacco in his mouth. "Think I've got it pretty well figured out."

John was silent for a moment, then spoke again. "I was thinking about the Indians. Can I tell you?"

Kohler spat and was silent.

"We've gone to considerable trouble here to work things out with the natives. And so far it's gone pretty well. You see, Brigham Young—president of the Church and governor of the territory—believes in treating the Indians fairly. He says we should feed them and clothe them and teach them how to farm. We haven't always done everything right in relating to the

Indians. But we're trying."

Sol listened to his father as he continued combing Star. He had heard plenty about their Indian policy, and he agreed with his father and with President Young. They were trying not only to be fair to the Indians, but to help them and civilize them.

An Indian practice that horrified Brigham Young was that of Indian braves raiding other Indian tribes for the purpose of taking their children to California or Mexico to be sold into slavery. Sometimes the Indian men even sold their own wives and children for firearms and horses. President Young felt that if the Indians insisted on selling their children, it would be best for the Mormons to purchase them and educate and Christianize them.

So the legislature had passed a law permitting Utah families to adopt children that Indian parents were determined to sell to the Mexicans. The law also ordered the arrest of roving bands of Mexicans who had come to purchase Indian slaves. Sol knew of two families that had taken Indian children in. President Young himself took care of several. One of them, whom he named Sally, was rescued from Chief Wanship's warriors, who were torturing her by cutting the fleshy parts of her legs and arms and thrusting firebrands into her wounds. She recovered and had lived in President Young's home for several years now.

"Well," said Kohler, spitting onto the straw floor of the barn, "as far as I can tell, bein' nice to the redmen is just askin' for trouble. They're mean through and through. The only good Injun is a dead Injun."

"But that's not so," objected John. "They're children of God just like the rest of us."

Kohler laughed out loud. "Injuns no more got souls than that there horse!"

Sol stopped his combing and frowned. No more soul than a horse? Didn't horses have souls? He'd never really thought about it. But a heaven without horses—that wouldn't be much of a heaven at all.

"I can't agree with you there, Mister Kohler. And I say that dealing with the Indians is like most everything else—what you give out is what you get back."

"But they're savages. First thing anybody builds out here is a fort."

"That's right. And we lived in it for a year or so before building our houses. The Indians expect violence. And they've got plenty to give. But once they learn that we're not out to kill them and cheat them, we can live in peace."

"Huh. That'll be a cold day in hell."

"Maybe so. Maybe so. But besides the fact that they're our brothers and deserve to be treated fairly, Brigham Young says it's cheaper to feed them than to fight them."

Kohler stood up and looked down at John coldly. "Well, we don't all have to believe what Brigham Young says, do we?"

John stood too and looked at Kohler evenly. "No. But we'd sure all be a lot better off if everybody did."

The two men started for the barn door. Reluctantly Sol stopped combing and put his lips against Star's ear. "I'll be back," he whispered. Then he stepped out of the stall, put the curry comb back on its hook, and followed the men.

Sol lay in bed that night looking out the window at the moon. He often stared at the moon, trying to figure out how and why it changed its form. It was amazing. It got big and bigger and then round and full, and then it got small and smaller, and then it wasn't there at all. How could that be? He knew about the reflection of the sun, but that didn't seem to explain everything. What was it all about? What was anything all about? He knew that he, like the moon, started out as almost nothing, and got bigger and bigger, and then, one of these days, he wouldn't be there at all. Dust to dust. What did it all mean? Would he come back like the moon? Or be somewhere else, at least? That's what he had been taught—that he was eternal and would appear in some other sky. But what about *now*?

Sol had been named after King Solomon in the Bible. The wise king. But Sol didn't always feel very wise. The only thing he had figured out for sure about life was that the Golden Rule made sense. But why didn't everybody else believe it and live it? Mister Kohler had been nice enough to him, but he'd just as soon shoot an Indian as look at one. Do unto others as you would have others do unto you—except for Indians. Was that it?

"You asleep, son?" The voice and a little light entered the dark room and came toward the bed.

"No, Pa."

Sol's father carried a candle, put it down on a little table, and sat on his son's bed. "What you thinking about?"

"Oh, things. Mister Kohler. And the Indians. And Star." He really had been thinking about Star. It's amazing how you can think of more than one thing at the same time. Ever since he had first seen her, Star had been there like a thin picture that lay over another picture, and he could see them both.

"You like that filly, huh?" John said, and then laughed at how much he sounded like Kohler.

"I *love* her," said Sol. He could use the word love with his father. His father would not laugh.

"I see."

"And do you know what?"

"What?"

Sol sat up a little. "I'm going to buy her. I'm going to work as hard as I can . . . doing anything I can for anybody that'll let me, and I'm going to buy her. If I get enough, Kohler'll sell her. I know he will."

John nodded slowly. "If you want her that bad, son."

"I do. I do." Sol lay back on his pillow and looked out again at the moon. "Pa? Do Indians really have souls?"

"Sure they do. Sure as you or I do."

"Why doesn't Mister Kohler think so?"

"Well, son, there's a lot of people who just can't bear not

to be better than somebody else. They've always got to have somebody lower down on the totem pole, so to speak. And if you can convince yourself that they belong down there—that they really aren't as good as you are—then you don't feel so guilty about it. Kohler doesn't want to treat the Indians well. So he has to believe that they don't really count."

"Oh."

"There's lots of injustice in the world, son. And the best thing you can do about it is to make sure that what *you* do is fair and right and honest. You can't decide what Nat Kohler will do. But you can decide what Sol McAllister will do." He reached for the candle and held it between himself and his son. "Look at this little light, son. And look at all the darkness out there. Doesn't seem to make much of a dent, does it? But listen here, and don't you forget it. All the darkness in the world cannot snuff out the light of this one little candle." John stood up. "You just keep on burning, and never mind all the Kohlers out there. Did you say your prayers?"

"Yes, Pa."

"Goodnight, son."

"Goodnight."

Sol went to sleep thinking about totem poles and candles and Kohler and the Indians and the moon. And Star.

CHAPTER THREE

"**P**a! Pa!" Sol ran toward his father as fast as his legs would carry him. John was drawing a bucket of water from the well and let the bucket fall back with a splash as he turned to his son. His ear had become well tuned to the voices of his livestock and the voice of his son, and he knew there was something wrong.

"What is it?"

"Indians! I think it's Arrowpine. They're just down the road riding this way like fury. Do you think they're on the warpath? Do you think . . . ?"

Sol could not even say what he was thinking. There hadn't been any big uprisings from the Indians for a while, but the Walker War four years ago in 1853 and 1854 was still fresh in their minds. It had started over the trading of three trout up in Springville. An Indian had begun beating his squaw for getting less than he thought she should have for the fish. A white man had tried to stop him. The Indian had grabbed the white man's gun, and the white man had hit the Indian over the head with the rifle barrel. The Indian had died. Soon Arrowpine's

brother, Chief Walker, had declared war on all white men. The
Utah militia was called out. And before it was finally settled,
nineteen white people and many Indians had been killed. Sol
knew that Arrowpine was their friend. But still . . .

John and Sol reached the front of the house just as Arrowpine rode up at full speed. Behind him were a squaw and three
braves. The squaw's black unbraided hair streamed loose
behind her, and the hair of the men was braided. Arrowpine
drew his horse to a halt and jumped off, landing without a
sound in the dusty road.

"You hide Arrowpine. Now!"

"Hide?" asked John. "From what?"

"Shoshonis. Shoshonis no friend to Arrowpine. Want to
kill. You hide."

Arrowpine motioned to the other Indians, who quickly
jumped from their horses.

"Sol, open the barn door quick!" called John.

Sol ran to the barn, opened the door, and stood back. The
Indians and John ran the horses into the barn, and Sol quickly
shut the door. Then they ran to the back door of the house and
entered.

Grandma and Paula looked up from the apples they were
paring for applesauce as they heard the door open.

"Oh, John, I wonder if you could . . ." Paula broke off in
mid-sentence as she saw five Indians run through the kitchen
and into the bedroom, followed by Sol.

Grandma lowered her paring knife slowly into her lap and
looked at Paula. "Was that . . . Indians?"

"Why, I . . . I think it was."

Immediately John and Sol reappeared and shut the door
to the bedroom.

"Don't move, either one of you. Don't move and don't say
a word no matter what."

John dashed for the door.

"John?" Grandma stood up and moved her pale blue eyes
from her son to the bedroom door. "Are there . . . Indians in

the bedroom?"

"There are. Now, don't move!" John and Sol quickly left the house, closing the door behind them.

Grandma slowly picked up her paring knife, reached for another apple, and kept her gaze on the bedroom door.

John and Sol had been outside only about a minute and a half when they heard the whoops and hoofbeats of the Shoshonis. Casually they continued chopping wood, looking up from their work only when the horses entered their yard.

Sol's stomach tightened as he looked at the wild faces of the ten Shoshoni braves, seated astride their sweating horses. The Indians wore only buckskin loin-cloths and mocassins, and their faces and bodies were stained from red berries. The leader's black eyes flashed as he demanded, "Where Arrowpine?"

John raised his right hand in a gesture of greeting. "Hello, Chief," he said.

"Where Arrowpine?" again demanded the Shoshoni chief. "He came here?"

Sol looked at his father and then at the Indian. How was his father going to handle this one with his philosophy of dealing honestly with the Indians?"

John McAllister looked around, as if for an idea. His eyes fixed on a small cloud of dust that rose from a spot in the road as it turned and disappeared over a little hill.

The Shoshoni chief followed his gaze and let out a whoop. His heels dug into his horse's flanks, and he jerked the horse around, urging it back to the road. The other Indians followed and off raced the band of whooping Shoshonis toward what they thought was the dust of their vanishing enemy.

Sol noticed that his knees were shaking, and he sat down on the woodpile. He looked over at his father and grinned.

"You believe in miracles, son?" said John, grinning back.

"Guess so."

John nodded his head. "You just saw one."

They continued chopping wood for a few minutes to make

sure the Shoshonis did not turn around and come back. Then
they went into the house. As they opened the door to the
kitchen, Grandma looked up from her apples.

"John . . . why are there Indians in the bedroom?"

Sol burst into laughter. It was a great relief to be able to
laugh. And seeing Grandma's innocent, amazed expression was
pretty funny.

"Well, I just invited them in for a while," said John. "Sort
of to save their lives."

Grandma nodded as if this made perfect sense and went
back to her paring.

"Is it all right?" asked Paula, going to the window and
looking out.

"I think so. Yes." John went to the bedroom and opened
the door. "You can come out now, Chief."

In a moment the kitchen was filled with five Indians.

"They came?" asked Arrowpine.

John nodded. "And went. You can thank the Great Spirit
for that. We were very lucky."

Arrowpine grunted. "Great Spirit good to Arrowpine.
John Mac good, too. Good friend."

"Now how do we get you out of here?"

"Shoshoni on both sides of valley. Many Shoshoni look
for Arrowpine. No good."

Sol spoke up suddenly. "Pa. What about the back of our
property? If you follow the creek far enough, you're out of the
valley. Sort of hard to find."

Arrowpine looked at John. "You take us there. We go
now."

"That might work," said John thoughtfully. "But like Sol
here says, it's pretty hard to find. I couldn't get you there and
be back before dark. And there's a meeting I've got to be to
tonight. The government's new Indian agent just arrived and
called a meeting of everybody who's interested in discussing
policy toward the Indians. I've got to be there. Too many
people—like Nat Kohler—don't care to give fair treatment to

you and your people, Arrowpine. I've got to be there to make sure a friendly voice is heard."

Arrowpine pointed to Sol. "*You* take us."

Paula drew in a quick breath and put down her paring knife. "Sol? Why he's . . . he's just a boy."

"I could do it," said Sol eagerly. "I know the pastures out there. I could do it easy. Can I, Pa?"

"Well . . ." John looked questioningly at his wife.

"Out there in the dark?" said Paula. "I don't think . . ."

Arrowpine interrupted. "Stay with Utes tonight. Come back tomorrow. Good."

Sol's eyes widened. Stay with the Indians? Sleep there? A delicious chill of terror and excitement ran down his spine. "I could, Ma," he said. "I'd be fine."

"I . . . I just don't know," said Paula helplessly. "I . . ."

"How old boy?" demanded Arrowpine's squaw, looking down at the white woman.

"I'm twelve," said Sol.

"My boy twelve," said the squaw. "My boy brave. All Ute boys brave. White boy baby."

Grandma's paring knife whanged into the cutting board as she stood up. Her pale blue eyes looked directly into the dark brown eyes of the squaw. "White boy not baby! White boy as brave as any Indian. Only he don't go out scalping people and . . ."

"Now, Grandma," said John, putting a hand on her shoulder.

"And what's more Sol is going to take them, and that's final!" She sat down indignantly and picked up her paring knife, scalping an apple with great energy.

"Can I, Ma? Can I?" pleaded Sol.

Paula nodded coolly and kept her eyes on her work, not wanting to betray the apprehension that rose in her in cold little waves.

They started out immediately, riding part of the way and then leading the horses as they came to the pass. Sol tried to make conversation with the chief, pointing out places of interest, like the spot where he had broken his leg two years ago when a horse shied and knocked him off into a gully.

"Look . . . these horses are ours. And the cows over there. You know how you can tell they're ours?"

The Indian did not reply.

"By the brand," Sol went on. "The 'M' with the bar under it. All our livestock have that. Nice horses, huh?"

Again the Indian did not reply. Undaunted, Sol continued. He had always had a remarkable gift for carrying on a conversation, even when the other party did not seem interested.

"But you know where the most beautiful horse in the world is? Over in the far pasture way over there. Her name is 'Star' and someday she's going to be mine."

They walked a little further in silence. They had been out now for three hours, and soon it would be getting dark. A warm breeze bounced a tumbleweed in front of them. The sky was pink where it touched the mountains, and the only sound that could be heard was hooves on soft soil.

"And here's the end of our property. We own a lot of land, huh?"

"You own *no* land." Arrowpine's face did not change expression, and he continued to look straight ahead.

"What do you mean? We're homesteading. It's ours!"

"White man own no land. Indian own no land. *All* land belong to Great Spirit."

"Oh." That was true, of course. Sol had been taught that everything was just here on loan from God. But he was surprised to hear Chief Arrowpine say it. "How do you know that?" he asked.

"My brother, Walker, he told me. He very great chief. Make white man afraid. Hate white man. He die. Arrowpine become chief. Hate white man more. Make white man more afraid. One night Walker come to Arrowpine from place where Great Spirit is chief. He say no fight Mormons. He say make peace with Mormons. He say land not belong to Indian or to white man. Land belong to Great Spirit."

Sol listened in astonishment. Arrowpine had had a *vision*? His brother had come to him from the spirit world to give him a message? Well, then, that proved it. Indians *did* have souls. He couldn't wait to tell Mister Kohler.

Abruptly Arrowpine took off the elk-tooth necklace he was wearing—the same one Sol had briefly owned—and placed it around Sol's neck.

"Good white boy," said the chief. "Help Arrowpine."

Sol grinned and felt the necklace with reverent fingers. "Thanks. Gee . . . thanks."

The lights of the Ute encampment were suddenly evident, and Sol felt a surge of relief. He was tired. Even a bed on the ground sounded good to him now.

"White boy hungry?" asked Arrowpine.

"Yes. I'm starving." Sol was suddenly ashamed as he said the word. He had never really known what it was to be starving. In spite of all the trials of pioneer living, he had always had something in his bowl for supper. But he knew that to the Indians starvation was a very real threat. Each winter many of them died of starvation, especially the Goshutes, a destitute tribe that was often reduced to stealing meat from the buzzards and the coyotes. Sol's father had told of seeing a group of these lean, scrawny creatures, too weak many of them even to chase the grasshoppers that provided supper.

Grasshoppers! Sol was not *that* starving. What if . . .

"Chief?" Sol's mother had instructed him never to inquire about food when he was a guest. It was rude, she had said. But she wasn't here now, and Sol was desperate. "Chief? What's for supper?"

Arrowpine looked at him blankly. "Food? Maybe squirrel. Maybe rabbit. What they catch today."

Sol had eaten rabbit. It wasn't too bad. And squirrel might be all right.

The Indians, squatting by the fire or beside their teepees,

stared at the white boy as he walked into the camp with their chief. After they tied up their horses, Arrowpine led Sol to his teepee, a conical shaped structure about fifteen feet in height and perhaps fifteen feet in diameter at the base. Buffalo skin covered the poles that were staked to the ground.

"Sit," demanded Arrowpine.

Sol lowered his weary body to the ground and leaned up against the teepee. He watched as Arrowpine's squaw poured into a bowl-shaped rock what looked like dark flour and water and made a thick mixture that she then cooked over the fire into little cakes. In a few minutes three of the cakes were thrust before Sol, and the squaw demanded, "Eat!"

Sol looked up at her and smiled politely. "Where's the squirrel?"

"Squirrel all gone. Eat."

Sol looked down at the dark cakes. "What . . . is it?"

"Grasshopper. Good."

The squaw went back to the fire, and Sol looked down at his supper. His stomach moved a little, and he leaned back and closed his eyes. He knew how they had prepared the grasshoppers. His father had told him. Grasshoppers were abundant in Utah, and in the fall when the weather became cold and the insects were numbed, the Indians gathered them in bushels. They then dug holes in the sand and heated stones in a fire. They covered a layer of hot stones with a layer of grasshoppers, continuing this until they had put them all on to roast. When the rocks were cool, they took the roasted insects from the hole and ground them into meal, putting much of it away to be used during the winter. Or maybe, Sol thought, to be served to unexpected guests when the squirrels had all been eaten.

Sol opened his eyes and looked again at the little cakes. He was hungry. But . . . still, you don't refuse food. His mother had always said, half-jokingly, "If you don't like what we're serving, you can just go to the neighbors and see if they'll feed you." Sol had never gone. And there were no neighbors out here. It was the grasshoppers — or nothing.

Well, nothing then. Sol had fasted before. Once each month the Mormons went without food for twenty-four hours, a practice that was supposed to strengthen the spirit and cleanse the body. He would just pretend that today was a fast day.

Slowly he took the little cakes, a piece at a time, ground them up between his thumb and his forefinger, and deposited them in the patch of grass at his left. Closer to the fire, Arrowpine and the other four braves were eating ravenously. Noticing that Sol's cakes were gone, the squaw came over with three more.

"You like grasshopper," she smiled. "You have more."

"No, no!" Sol said, holding his palms out in protest and shaking his head. "That was plenty. I'm really . . . full."

"White boy skinny. Have more." And the squaw plopped the cakes in front of him, turning back to the fire.

Cautiously Sol looked around for another patch of grass.

Sol slept without difficulty. The rabbit-skin robe under him and the rabbit-skin robe over him were comfortable, and the crickets' familiar melody lulled him easily to sleep. He was just outside Arrowpine's teepee, and the bright stars overhead gradually blurred and disappeared as his tired eyes closed.

The first sound Sol heard the next morning was the tap of a drum. He opened his eyes and raised up on one elbow to see what was happening. Chief Arrowpine was leading a young Indian maiden out into a nearby clearing. Behind them walked at least two dozen Indian braves, divided into two groups. The drum stopped, and the Indian braves lined up facing one another in silence.

Sol threw the rabbit-skin robe off and quickly put on his shoes. He ran to the clearing and made his way to the side of Chief Arrowpine. As he arrived, the drum tapped again, and the two lines of Indian braves, with bowed heads and arms wildly beating the air, rushed like angry animals upon each other. For a few moments they continued beating the air, and then at the second tap of the drum they clenched, the mass becoming a seething, whirling cyclone of dark figures. On the sidelines, the squaws cheered and on-looking warriors gave an occasional war-whoop.

Sol looked up anxiously at Arrowpine. "What are they doing?"

Arrowpine's eyes were fastened on the scene before him. "Fight for Arrowpine daughter."

Sol glanced at the slender, delicate-looking girl whose brown eyes were wide in fear as she watched the warriors. "Why?" he asked.

"Time to marry. Two braves want girl, pay same number of ponies. Indian custom settle who wins. Ankawakeets big. Panimeto no big. Cannot fight. Twenty warriors fight for each brave. If Ankawakeets' braves win, he wins. If Panimeto's win, he wins."

Stunned, Sol looked at the warriors, viciously throwing each other to the ground.

"Who keeps the other down for time it takes to scalp, he wins," said Arrowpine.

"But . . . but . . ." Sol's face was troubled. "The girl . . . who does *she* want?"

Arrowpine looked at the boy as if his question did not make sense. "She want? Panimeto. No matter. If Panimeto braves win, he have her." Arrowpine's attention went back to the fight.

Fascinated, Sol stood beside the chief and watched. An Indian boy about his age stood on the other side of the chief next to the girl. That would be the chief's son, the one the squaw had said was braver than the white boy. He wore an elk-tooth necklace identical to the one Arrowpine had given Sol. He was slightly taller than Sol and stood protectively beside the girl, anxiously looking from her to the fighting braves.

After the battle had continued for about an hour, Arrowpine signaled, and the sound of the drum was heard above the whoops of the warriors. The Indian braves let go of their opponents and stepped back into two lines, panting. Only one warrior from each side had been vanquished. Arrowpine then spoke quickly in Ute, and the lines moved further apart. The Indian girl fell on her knees and grabbed her father's hand. Tears streamed down her lovely brown face as she pled with him. Sol could not understand her words, but he understood her anguish. What did it mean? He glanced at her brother, who had turned away and put his face in his hands. Sol looked at Arrowpine's squaw, who stood watching it all, unmoved. She was older than the young people. She had been seasoned to the customs of the tribe and did not question any more. Her arms were folded over the front of her leather dress, and her weathered face betrayed no emotion as she watched Arrowpine lead her daughter into the midst of the waiting warriors. Arrowpine's face was also without emotion. He led his daughter with the same authority that he led his horse.

Sol watched as two of the warriors stepped out and faced one another. Those must be the contenders for Arrowpine's daughter. The other braves lined up behind the two, grasping each other solidly around the waist. Arrowpine placed his daughter between Ankawakeets and Panimeto and stepped back. The girl had stopped crying now, and she lifted her face to the sky as if for strength. Then she raised her arms and extended a hand to each of the braves.

Was it possible? Sol stepped back and suddenly felt dizzy. They wouldn't . . . Arrowpine couldn't . . . The chief, as if performing a ceremony, marked lines in the sand, and then stood back. He signaled again, and the sound of the drum was heard. The two braves at the head of each line slowly reached out with both hands and grasped a wrist of the trembling maiden. Another signal from Arrowpine. Another roll of the drum. The lines began to move, swaying back and forth like a snake that can't make up its mind which way to go. The girl cried out, then bowed her head, and was silent.

Sol had seen tug of wars before. He had been in them. Just

a few weeks ago at the big celebration, his side had won, and they had all gotten ice cream. But they were pulling on a rope, not a . . . a human being.

The girl danced wildly, first in one direction and then in the other as the two sides took the advantage, then lost it. Sol felt sick. This wasn't happening. It couldn't be happening. The girl . . . could be killed. She could be torn apart! Sol ran a few feet back to a small tree and grasped the trunk as his body wretched. There was nothing to come up, as he'd had no supper, but he wretched again and again, hanging onto the tree.

He looked over at the contest. One of the wild swirls of the warriors brought them to the banks of a creek, where they fell in the water up to their necks. The girl was entirely submerged, only her mass of glossy tresses floating on the surface of the water. Sol glanced at Arrowpine. Surely he wouldn't let them . . . But Arrowpine made no move to interfere. Suddenly the girl's brother darted from his place and leaped into the creek, grasping the girl's hair and pulling her face above the water. Instantly every brave broke his hold and scrambled up onto the banks, Ankawakeets and Panimeto shouting angrily at the boy. The young Indian led his gasping sister up onto the banks.

Arrowpine approached the two children, speaking harshly to the boy and gesturing to the teepees. The boy bowed his head and left the scene of the battle.

Sol wanted to run to Arrowpine, to beg the chief to let the girl go. But if he wouldn't listen to his own children, surely he wouldn't listen to a white boy. Custom was stronger than the desires of a young girl's heart, stronger even than the affection of a father. Centuries of tribal practice stood behind Arrowpine like an army with spears as he took his daughter's hand again and led her back to the center of the field.

Sol could watch no longer. He turned and ran as fast as he could up the hill. He didn't stop as he heard the tap of the drum. He didn't stop as he heard the whooping of the warriors as they resumed their battle. He ran, still dizzy, up the side of the hill. But just as he reached the summit, Sol heard a loud cheer and roll of the drum from the valley below, and he stopped and looked back.

The two lines were broken now, and the young girl lay in a heap on the ground at the foot of the larger Indian. Ankawa- keets was the victor! He held his arms above his head in triumph. Arrowpine walked to his daughter, lifted her to her feet, and presented her to the smiling Indian. So he had won his bride. Panimeto walked away. Sol was still close enough to see the girl's face as she watched the one she loved leave the field. The pain of her body and the pain of her heart were over- whelming. And again Sol turned and ran.

It felt good to be in his father's pastures. He stopped running and sat down in the tall green grass to rest. Would he ever forget that look on the face of the trembling girl? Where was the justice? Was she only property to be fought over? Where was the Golden Rule? Would the Indian braves like to be treated as they had treated the girl?

Sol remembered a few years ago when he heard the men talking about the Indian custom of killing a brave's squaw and his horses when the brave died so he would have company going to the red men's world of spirits. Sol had innocently asked if the squaw's husband and horses were killed to go with her when she died. The men had laughed and hit each other on the back as if they had heard a great joke. Sol had not understood why they had laughed. But he was beginning to understand.

Everyone seemed to have someone that didn't count as much as they counted. White men had Indians. Indian braves had Indian squaws. It was all very confusing. He would talk to Grandma about it sometime.

Sol got up and continued his journey home. He hoped that the Mormon leaders would soon convince the Indians to give up the brutal custom of the squaw fight. But now, as he walked home through the clear July morning—and always as his memory brought it back from time to time—Sol remembered with chilling detail the look on the face of the young Indian maiden as she raised her arms and looked to the sky.

CHAPTER FOUR

Sol pulled out from under his bed the little carved wooden box that Grandma had given him and dusted it off. He dumped out the collection of fool's gold, shiny little rocks that looked like real gold nuggets, and put the box carefully on the bright quilt. This would be his bank. And he would fill it with coins until there was enough to buy Star. More than enough. And Kohler would not be able to resist. She was just another horse to him.

Holding the box, Sol walked out into the kitchen, where his mother and grandmother were finishing the supper dishes and his father was cleaning his rifle. John did not like having a gun in the house, but out here on the frontier it seemed a necessity. Sometimes John brought home a pheasant or a duck or a rabbit, and they ate it for supper. Sol remembered his father saying that he never shot game without a prayer of thanksgiving that the Lord had provided for the sustaining of life. He never shot out of malice or just for sport.

And, too, the gun was essential because being out here in Indian territory, they were constantly on the edge of danger.

Every once in a while Sol heard a story that made him shiver. Just a few months ago a whole family had been killed by Indians who were out to get the first whites they saw after one of their own had been gunned down for stealing corn. The rifle was kept in a secret place under a plank in his parents' bedroom, and they had all been instructed in its use, even Grandma. Sol's mother had insisted that she would never use the rifle, even if her life were threatened. And Sol wondered if he would. Could he ever take aim at another human being?

"Pa?"

"Yes, son?" John looked up from the rifle.

"How much do you think it'll take to buy Star?"

"Well, that's hard to say. Maybe fifteen dollars. Maybe more, maybe less."

"I'll offer him twenty."

"Twenty dollars?" asked Grandma, looking at him with an expression of disbelief. "Where you goin' to get twenty dollars?"

"Work for it. Pa said I can do my jobs here in the early morning and in the evening. I'll hire out—do what anybody needs to have done. Plough. Cut hay. Load wood. I'm strong. Look at that there muscle, Grandma."

Sol flexed the muscle of his right arm for Grandma, who reached out a tentative finger.

"Don't know if I should touch it," she said. "Might pop it."

Sol hollered and laughed as he grabbed Grandma like a sack of potatoes and lifted her up off the floor. Grandma shrieked in delight and pounded him on the back with her fists. "Hey, now! Put me down, you hear?"

"Sol!" exclaimed his mother laughing.

"So what were you saying about my muscles, Grandma?" asked Sol. "That they're about the biggest, strongest muscles you ever saw?"

"That's just what I was sayin'," chortled Grandma.

"Probably the biggest muscles a twelve year old boy ever

had?"

"Probably so . . . on both sides of the Mississippi."

"And that I can easy hire out and earn me twenty dollars?"

"Easy!"

Sol gently let Grandma slip to the floor. "That's what I thought you said." Sol was a good three inches taller than his Grandma, and he looked down at her and smiled.

"In fact," said Grandma, walking to the cupboard and taking down a dish, "here's twenty-five cents to start things movin'. And when you get that horse, I get to take her out for a trot."

"You bet!"

Sol opened the little box and smiled as the coin thudded against the wood. "Thanks, Grandma."

"Say, you know who might be needing a hand, son?" John leaned the rifle up against the wall and looked at Sol.

"Who?"

"Mr. Kohler. Did you notice all those fences he was putting in? Looks like he's big on fences. Bet he could use some help digging post holes."

Sol smiled. "I'll go see him tomorrow."

Fifty-seven. And the next one would be fifty-eight. Sol looked back at the line of post holes, and his muscles — his incredibly strong muscles, stronger probably than those of any twelve year old boy on both sides of the Mississippi — screamed with exhaustion. He took a swallow of water from his buckskin canteen and sat down, leaning his back against a large rock.

This was his first day working for Mr. Kohler. Kohler had been happy to hire him for fifty cents a day. It sounded good to Sol when they talked about it. But now after digging fifty-seven post holes in the July sun, he wasn't sure. He took another swallow of water and thought about Star. She was worth it. She was worth anything he had to do to get her.

Maybe Sol wouldn't have needed a horse of his own so

badly if he hadn't been an only child. He didn't used to be an only child. His younger brother and sister had died a few years ago of scarlet fever. And he had almost died himself. He remembered that after the funeral the house felt so quiet. And Sol felt so alone. He still felt alone. He loved his mother and father, and he loved Grandma. But they were grownups, and Sol needed a friend. There were boys his age in the settlement, and he saw them every week at church and on other occasions. But there was nobody he wanted to spend hours and hours with — even if he'd had the hours to spend. All his longings for a brother, sister, friend had rolled themselves up into one creature. Star. He knew that once Star was his — once he could ride her any time he wanted — once she was really his, he would never be alone again.

That was worth fifty-seven post holes. That was worth a thousand post holes and more. Sol stood up and picked up the shovel. Just twenty more, and then he'd walk back to the barn and give Star a good brushing.

Sol was just approaching the barn when he saw the door fly open and Mr. Kohler lead the big white stallion out into the sunlight. In one hand was his rifle. The tight set of his mouth and the speed with which he mounted the animal told Sol that Kohler was probably not going out pheasant hunting.

"Mr. Kohler! What's the matter?" Sol ran the remaining distance to the barn.

"Damn Injun thief. I'll kill 'im!"

"Indians?" Sol looked around. There was not a trace of anything unusual on the landscape.

"Stole clothes off the line. Stole my best plaid shirt. The missus saw 'im and came in screamin'. I'll get the damn Injun thief!"

Mr. Kohler pressed his knees into the horse's flesh, and the animal broke into an instant gallop.

"But Mr. Kohler! Don't . . . You can't . . . ." Sol was about to tell Mr. Kohler what he'd heard his father say a hundred or more times — that you can't solve the Indian problem by killing them, even when they do something wrong. But his voice was drowned by the pounding of the horse's hoofs. And Mr. Kohler would not have listened anyway. Sol knew that he wasn't used to listening, especially to people shorter than he was. So he watched Kohler ride off, his rifle barrel glinting in the sun.

Propping the shovel in its place in the barn, Sol tried to decide what to do. He wanted to ride home and alert his father that there might be trouble. But John was away for the day. Better to just stay here and find out what was going to happen.

Mr. Kohler wouldn't really kill the Indian, would he? Wouldn't he just arrest him? Sometimes Indians were tried like white people.

Sol climbed through the wooden slats of the stall and put his arms around Star's sleek neck.

"Hi, Star. You okay, huh?"

The filly whinnied and nuzzled her warm nose into Sol's chest. Sol laid his cheek onto the white star and sighed. Why couldn't human beings be as smart as horses? Horses wouldn't go out with guns to kill each other. Well, they fought sometimes. Wild horses battled over mares, he knew that. And he had seen two giant deer lock antlers just last year, and one of them had gotten ripped up pretty bad. But weren't humans supposed to be better and higher than animals? Didn't the Lord make humans *after* the animals when he'd had all that practice and could really do the job right? So why did humans go after each other with rifles? Sol sighed again and picked up the curry comb.

Less than an hour later Sol heard an approaching horse and ran out of the barn to see Mr. Kohler riding up. Sol felt the blood surge in his veins as he watched the horse and rider come closer. The barrel of the rifle, pointed toward the sky, had something draped over it. But that wasn't what caused Sol's heart almost to stop beating. It was the look of triumph on Mr. Kohler's face. He was grinning so wide that his slit eyes were almost closed.

"Got 'im," he cried.

Sol opened his mouth to speak, but he could not. Got him? He watched in horror as the large man got down from his horse, holding a rifle over which was draped like a flag a plaid shirt. Sol's eyes widened as he saw a deep red stain on the fabric.

"Damn Injun ruined my shirt—got two bullet holes right through it."

Sol stumbled toward his father's horse and quickly untied the reins. "I . . . I got to go home."

Sol leapt onto the back of the gray mare and urged her toward the road.

"You finished them post holes?" Kohler called after him.

Sol urged the horse on, faster and faster. Kohler did not understand. He had killed an Indian. As soon as the tribe found out about it, there was sure to be trouble. Sol had to get home as fast as he could to warn his mother and Grandma. They'd better stay inside and bolt all the doors.

Sol had been riding about fifteen minutes when he heard the whoops. He didn't turn around and began to pray as hard as he could that he was just hearing things. But they came again —the unmistakable whoops of Indians behind him.

Sol glanced back, and what he saw filled him with terror. At least a dozen Indian braves, dark unpainted skin shining in the sun, were coming toward him. Their black heads leaned in over the backs of their ponies like arrows heading for the target.

Digging his knees deeper into the sides of the mare, Sol leaned down close to the horse's body. If they were going to shoot arrows, he'd be safer this way. Were they the friends of the Indian Mr. Kohler had killed? Did they think he had done it? But the Indians didn't really care who had done it, did they? Their minds didn't work that way. A white man had done it, and the first white man they found would pay for it.

Closer and closer came the sound of the horses' hoofs and the yelping of the Indians behind him. Only one more mile, and he'd be home. Then a bigger fear seized his heart. Would they kill not only him, but his mother and grandmother? He made the decision in an instant and turned the horse onto the road that led toward town. It was five miles. He'd never get there, but he wouldn't endanger anybody else.

Two Indian braves were approaching on either side of him. Sol had been going at full speed, but the Indian ponies were faster. Sol's eyes went from side to side as the two braves came abreast of him, not even glancing at him, and then moved on ahead. Their faces were set and emotionless. Sol could barely breathe, but again he urged the mare on. And prayed.

When the Indians were a few feet in front of him, both braves, as if on signal, moved in toward each other, directly in the path of Sol's horse. They slowed down a little. Sol's horse was forced to slow. Then two other braves rode up on either side of him, leaned over, and each grabbed him by an arm and a leg. Sol felt himself being lifted from the saddle. His horse was moving out from under him! He was straddling air, held up by the strong, bronze arms of the Indian braves.

Then all of a sudden Sol felt the hands leave him. In an instant he was on the ground, rolling over and over in the dust. Hoofbeats pounded in his ears. He opened his eyes and looked back. An Indian pony was upon him—over him. The white belly of the horse streaked above him like a flash of lightning. Sol pulled himself into a ball and closed his eyes. Another horse passed over him. And another.

The hoofbeats grew softer, and after a few moments Sol opened his eyes and slowly and painfully lifted himself up on one elbow. The Indians were thundering along the road ahead of him, without looking back. With the gray mare. The mare! That's what they wanted! They didn't want him at all—they wanted his horse!

Slowly Sol rose to his knees, then to his feet. His legs held. His arms were not broken. His head pounded with a tremendous ache, and he could feel blood trickling from his forehead. There was blood, too, on his elbows. But he was alive. And he was all right. And the Indians were gone. Thank God! It was a short prayer, but Sol had never been more sincere. He turned around and slowly began the walk home.

It was hard, but Sol managed not to cry out as his mother scrubbed the dirt from his wounds. All over his arms and his knees and the left side of his face were places where the skin had been scraped off. Then Grandma applied mineral water with a little flannel cloth. She used mineral water for everything from sore throats to indigestion. And especially wounds. It was cool anyway, and it felt good on the abrasions that burned like he had fallen into a fire.

"How you feeling, son?" John leaned over Sol and looked at him, forcing a smile.

Sol forced a smile back and said, "All right. I'm sorry, Pa. . . . about the mare. After I finish earning Star, I'll save up and get you another horse."

"No, son, that's not needful."

"Sol." Paula's voice was pleading. "Please don't go back there. I don't trust Mr. Kohler, especially after today. I don't even want you on his property."

"Ma, I've got to. I've got to get Star away from there. She can't be happy with him. I've got to, Ma."

Paula sighed and turned away. John pulled up a stool and sat down close to Sol.

"Not for a couple of weeks, you don't, son. Tomorrow you won't even be able to move. And until we see if there's going to be more trouble with the Indians, I don't want you to leave the place. They've been pretty unhappy about the white man moving closer and closer to the lake. We signed a treaty.

We promised to leave them their best hunting grounds near the lake. But we don't keep our word, even some of the Mormons. We push them further and further. And they feel they have no recourse but to steal from us. Isn't that what we've been doing to them, stealing the land they've been on for hundreds of years?"

Sol nodded, and just the silent motion made his head pound. "What's the answer, Pa? Should we just never have come?"

"No. We were pushed out of our lands back in Illinois. There was room for everybody if we'd all have just tried harder to get along and forget our differences. And there's room enough here—if we could all just exercise a little tolerance and cooperation—if we'd all be fair and honest. But that doesn't seem to happen hardly anywhere in the world—except for short periods of time. Still, you got to try for it. You just got to."

The Golden Rule. Would it ever work, Sol wondered? It was miles and miles up the road and would the human race ever get there? Where they were now was "Do unto others as others do unto you." You move onto their land. They steal your shirt and your corn. You shoot them. They shoot back.

Sol closed his eyes, and the pounding in his head continued. Like horses' hoofs. Behind him. Around him. Over him. Horses' hoofs, beating and beating on the dusty road. Finally, he slept.

CHAPTER FIVE

Sol studied Kohler's face for any sign of fear as they sat there in the room that served as the town hall. How could he look so calm? Also in the room were John McAllister and a few other settlers from nearby farms, Chief Arrowpine and the squaw and sons of the Indian who had been killed.

"Indian saw!" Arrowpine pointed a finger forcefully at Kohler. "He shoot Red Eagle!"

Kohler held out both hands in a gesture of helplessness. "Chief, it was an accident! I saw something moving in the grass. I thought it was a wolf! I didn't mean to kill no Injun!"

Lying must get easier the more you do it, thought Sol as he watched Mr. Kohler. And Mr. Kohler must have lied an awful lot to do it so well. If Sol hadn't seen him jump on his horse and go out after the Indian, he might have believed what he was hearing now. Sol glanced over at his father. They had already talked and decided it would be of no use for Sol to confront Kohler and accuse him of lying. Doing what they could to satisfy the Indians without violence was more important.

Arrowpine stood to his full six feet and looked down at Kohler. "You kill Red Eagle." Then he gestured at the squaw and Indian boys. "Red Eagle squaw—children—no have brave! Maybe die in snow!"

John McAllister spoke. "Now, Chief, I think this can be worked out. We're mighty grateful that you would meet with us on the problem instead of sending out your warriors to kill Mr. Kohler. We're mighty grateful for that, aren't we, Mr. Kohler?"

Nat Kohler nodded, shifting uneasily in his chair.

"And I think we can work this out to your satisfaction. Mr. Kohler is my neighbor, and I believe he wants to deal fairly and justly."

Sol stared at his father. Was he hearing the first lie that had ever crossed his father's lips? Or was his father just sort of . . . hoping? Sol had heard his father say, "If you treat a man the way he is, he'll stay that way, but if you treat him the way he ought to be, that's what he'll become." Nat Kohler—fair and just?

Sol's father went on. "I believe he wants to do the right thing—knowing that an unhappy Indian is a scalping Indian."

"Why, shore, shore," said Kohler with a nervous enthusiasm.

"And I believe Mr. Kohler will want to provide for the departed brave's family against the coming winter. Am I right, Mr. Kohler?"

Kohler glowered at John for a moment, then settled back into his chair and spoke darkly. "Guess so."

"How does one ox and two hundred pounds of flour sound, Chief?"

Kohler sat up abruptly. "An Ox?"

"Two ox!" said Arrowpine. "And three hundred pounds flour. And . . . food for all Indians."

"Huh?" Kohler looked at the chief. "You crazy?"

"A feast! What a great idea, Chief. I'm sure Mr. Kohler will be happy to provide a feast for all the Indians that want to come. A feast at his place! Nothing keeps friendship alive like sharing good food. What a fine idea!"

Kohler opened his mouth, but no words came. Sol had never seen him at a loss for words, and he had to hide a smile.

Arrowpine stood up. "Good. Tomorrow. We come tomorrow."

The other Indians followed the chief out of the room, and the white settlers looked at one another and smiled.

"Count yourself lucky, Kohler," said Jenkins Broadhead, the man who had refereed the wrestling. "Arrowpine hasn't been any too fond of you since you two met. If you value that there hair that's growing out of your scalp, I suggest you put on a right fine feed."

"We'll all help," added John. "You kill the fatted calf, and we'll help cook it. And we'll bring the brass band."

Following the men from the room, Sol looked back at Nat Kohler, still sitting in his chair, eyes almost shut, cracking his knuckles, and breathing a little harder than you would expect of a man just sitting in a chair.

Sol would always remember the next day, the feast day. He remembered about two hundred Indians on ponies arriving at Mr. Kohler's place. He remembered Red Eagle's squaw and children sitting at a table of honor and receiving the condolences of the white neighbors. He remembered the smell of the roasting calves and the spattering of the grease as the animals were turned on the spits over the fires. He remembered watching the band playing and the men singing "Rally 'Round the Flag, Boys," and then the men and women dancing. But most of all he remembered—and he would never forget—Nat Kohler with a large white apron over his belly, carrying huge trays of beef and mutton and potatoes and pies, and serving them to the Indians seated on benches and rocks and the ground in his own farmyard.

Sol watched much of the activities from the barn as he

brushed Star.

"Look at that, Star. Would you look at that? Bet that's a sight you'll never see again as long as you live."

Sol vigorously brushed the short black hair of Star's neck and smiled.

A treaty had been signed. Arrowpine had been approached a few days after the feast, when he still remembered the taste of the white man's mutton, and agreed that all past wrongs would be forgotten, and red men and white men would pledge to work together for peace. The red men would not steal livestock or other things belonging to the white men, and the white men would stay clear of the Indians' hunting territory, especially the land near to the lake. And there would be no shooting.

Sol continued digging post holes until the ground froze in December. He did a little work for other nearby settlers, but mostly he worked for Nat Kohler. And the coins went into the little box, making it fuller and fuller. Every night Sol would sit on the side of his bed and count the coins by the light of an oil lamp. He stacked them in rows, made designs of them, counted them, and counted them again. When he had enough, he arranged them on the table in the shape of a horse. One leg was very short, and there wasn't much tail, but by next week — by next week he would just about have enough to buy Star. What if he could get Star for Christmas? Maybe he could help some of the men load wood. They were still bringing down firewood from the mountains to see them through what might be a long winter. He'd ask around tomorrow at church.

They were just climbing into the wagon to set out for church when Jenkins Broadhead rode up fast on his brown and white horse.

"No church today, John," he said as he hastily

dismounted.

No church? It took flood or fire to make the Mormons cancel a church meeting. The only time Sol remembered it happening was when Brigham Young dismissed conference and sent the people home to put together provisions and wagons to go rescue a handcart company that was dying on the plains of Wyoming, stuck in an early winter storm. That was religion, Brigham had said, to go bring in the people on the plains, and he wanted them to go now!

"What's happening, Jenkins?" asked John.

"A posse's leaving in a half an hour. Fifty cattle were stolen during the night by the Indians. They're caught in the canyon. Some of the settlers are all for going up and killing the thieves. We asked Captain Smith to send out a posse to bring 'em back, give 'em a trial, show 'em how civilized people deal with lawbreakers. He said to go shoot 'em. We said no. Finally he agreed to have us bring 'em back here. Come with us, John. We need you to help keep the men cool."

"Of course." John jumped down from the wagon. "Let me just change clothes first."

"Can I go, Pa?" asked Sol. "I could help talk if you need more talkers. I talk real good."

"You sure do," laughed Jenkins. "We all noticed that."

"Not if there's danger up there, John," said Paula quickly. "That's no place for a boy."

"I'm almost thirteen, Ma. Please."

John considered a moment. "I think I'd like him to go, Paula. Sol has to learn how these things are done. One of these days it's going to have to be up to him to keep peace with the Indians."

Sol jumped off the wagon and headed for the house, unbuttoning his white Sunday shirt.

As they approached the canyon, it began to snow. Large, white flakes appeared and then melted on the reddish-brown neck of the horse Sol was riding.

"Can't be much further," said Jenkins. "We got four men

at the other end, so the Indians can't get out that way."

In half an hour the snow had stopped melting as it touched the ground, and a thin, white blanket was everywhere. Suddenly the man in the lead reined in his horse.

"There they are!"

Sol stood up in the stirrups and looked. Over to the left by a large clump of cottonwood trees was a small band of six Indians, sitting on the ground, waiting. Suddenly Sol thought of the handcart company, sitting in the snow, waiting for help. Nearby, grazing on the meager grass was the herd of fifty cattle, their hides bearing the unmistakable brand of the white man.

They rode closer, and Sol could see the helpless, hopeless eyes of the Indians. Twenty-five white men with rifles. Sol guessed there was probably not one Indian that expected to live until sundown.

John McAllister got off his horse and walked toward the red men. The posse had elected him spokesman, knowing that he had a way with the Indians. A tall brave walked to meet John.

"Indians have white man's cattle," said John. "That is no good. Indians follow us to town where we will have a trial."

"No," said the tall Indian. "Shoot us here. No shoot us in town."

"We're not going to shoot you at all. But there will perhaps be a punishment. No one can steal. Come with us to town."

"No." The Indian took a step backwards. "No trust white man. White man take to town to shoot Indian. Other white man watch and laugh."

John stepped closer to the Indian. "We will *not* shoot you — here or in town. I am John Mac, a good friend of Arrowpine, and he trusts me. I promise you on my own life that you will not be killed. Arrowpine promised you would not steal. We will have a trial, and we will invite Arrowpine. Justice will be done, but we will not shoot you. I promise."

The Indian studied John, studied the men on horses

behind him, then turned and spoke for a few moments in Ute
to the other Indians. Then he turned again to John.

"We go."

When they arrived at the military post, Captain Smith was
there to meet them. His well-brushed blond hair reached past
the collar of his faded blue uniform. Cold blue eyes were set in
a handsome bearded face.

"These the cattle thieves?" he asked sharply.

"They are," nodded John.

"Bring them over here," Smith gestured to the side of the
barracks.

John spoke to the Indians, and they obediently went
toward the building. Then they turned around and watched as
the captain spoke again.

"Shoot them!"

John whirled around to face the captain. "What?"

Captain Smith took a step toward John. "You don't hear
so good? I said shoot them!"

"We can't. We won't! I promised them safety. I promised
them a trial. With the chief here."

"There will be no trial." The captain spoke slowly and
deliberately. "This posse exists under my authority. I have been
empowered by the government of the United States of America
to deal with the Indians as I see fit. And I see fit to shoot
them." He leaned in and his face was just a few inches from
John's. "Do you understand?"

John did not move. His eyes looked directly into those of
the captain. "I understand. And we will not shoot the Indians."

Captain Smith turned to the men, color rising in his face.
"Shoot them!" he shouted.

No one moved.

With an oath, Captain Smith grabbed a rifle from a
nearby man and cocked it. Sol nearly cried out as he saw his
father place a hand on the barrel of the gun.

"I don't think you ought to do that, Captain," he said slowly. "Because if you kill anybody, you're going to have to kill me first. I promised these Indians safety. And if I can't keep that promise, I'd just as soon die with them."

The Indians stared dumbly as John walked toward them, turned, and stood in front of them, looking calmly at Captain Smith.

The captain half-raised his rifle, then lowered it. For a long moment the two men stared at one another, neither looking away, neither blinking.

Finally the captain spoke between clenched teeth. "Lock them up."

"Feed them first," said John.

Captain Smith turned angrily to his lieutenant. "I said lock them up!"

John spoke again, more quietly than before. "Feed them first."

Turning on his heel, the captain spat out the words, "Feed them!"

John turned to the Indians. "Follow me," he said.

Sol began again to breathe as he watched his father lead the Indians to a wooden shed. And years later, as Sol looked back on the events of that Sunday, he was certain that of all the sermons he had ever heard or seen, this one was the best.

Sol held Grandma steady as she stood on a chair and wound the strings of popcorn around the tall pine tree they had hauled down from the mountain.

"Here. Better let me do the star," said Sol as he helped her down from the chair. In his hand he held the bright gold star that had been the one "unnecessary" that Grandma had brought with her when they moved from the East. Sol had always believed it was pure gold, but after he learned it was just brass, he loved it anyway. As soon as Grandma's star was on the tree, the season really became Christmas.

And as soon as Sol's Star was here, it would be Christmas all year long. Yesterday and the day before, he helped Brother Farr haul wood. And now he had it—right there in the box—twenty dollars. Tomorrow was Christmas Eve, and in the morning, he'd just go over to Mr. Kohler and offer the money to him for Star. He wouldn't refuse twenty dollars.

Twenty dollars! And Sol had even taken a little money to buy some factory cloth for a dress for his mother and for Grandma and a shirt for his father. And gold buttons for the eyes of the rag doll he and Paula were making for Grandma. Grandma never tired of talking of the wonderful dolls she'd had on the plantation in North Carolina, and Sol and his mother decided this Christmas would be a good time to give Grandma a doll. Every day she seemed to get a little more child-like, and they thought she'd love to have a little doll to put on her bed.

"Peace on earth, goodwill to men," sang Grandma, in a high, wavering voice.

"Well, we do have peace for Christmas," said Paula, as she added a few homemade ornaments to the green branches. "At least this week we do."

Again Sol was grateful that his father and the other settlers had prevented a major Indian uprising. The trial had been held. Arrowpine was present and had suggested a punishment that the white settlers agreed to. The cattle thieves were whipped and promised to steal no more.

"Sing with me, Sol," said Grandma. "Silent night . . . holy night . . ."

Sol and Paula joined in. This was their favorite Christmas song, and they'd been singing it every day for two weeks now. "Sleep in heavenly peace. Sleep in . . ."

The door swung open, and all three turned as a gust of cold air and John McAllister entered the room. Heavenly peace was not written on his face. Deep concern was written there.

"What is it, John?" Paula could read her husband's face even better than Sol could.

"They shot twelve Indians!" John exploded. "They were caught with white men's cattle, and Captain Smith lined them up and shot them himself."

"Oh, no!" Paula sank down on the little couch, putting a hand to her mouth.

John slammed his fist onto the table. "We signed a treaty! We promised we would not shoot the Indians. Such fools! Can't they see? No telling what the tribe's going to do now. No telling!"

Grandma reached out and took her son's hand. John drew her close.

"Good thing you've got me around to cuss for you once in a while, son," said Grandma. "*Damn* Captain Smith!"

A faint smile crossed John's lips. "Thank you, Grandma. Thank you."

As the others watched in silence, Sol climbed onto the chair and slowly placed Grandma's gold star at the very, very top of the tree.

CHAPTER SIX

Corn meal mush was never Sol's favorite. But it tasted a little better with just a tiny sprinkling of sugar on it. The Jamesons had given them a whole cup of white sugar to help them celebrate Christmas, and they were going to make it last as long as they could.

Sol and Grandma and Paula ate breakfast in silence. John was already up and gone. At the crack of dawn he had taken off for the Ute encampment to find Arrowpine and try to talk him into keeping his braves under control. The shooting of twelve Indians would be a hard thing to explain.

Paula threw down her spoon. "Why does *he* always have to be the one to go? Isn't that what they appointed Indian agents for? Why can't *they* go?"

But she knew the answer to her question. And Sol and Grandma knew that she knew, so they just kept on eating their corn meal mush and did not reply. The Indian agents *wouldn't* go in the first place, wouldn't risk their lives to approach Arrowpine on his own territory. And even if they did, Arrowpine wouldn't listen to them. He didn't trust them. And he trusted John Mac. That's why John always had to be the one to go.

Paula picked up her spoon again and absently stirred a little more milk into her mush. "He might never even get there."

"He'll get there," said Grandma, putting a soothing hand on Paula's arm.

"But the Indians are angry!"

"They know John is a friend of Arrowpine's."

"But they might shoot an arrow before they even know *who* he is."

That was true. Sol and Grandma were quiet. They had prayed for John along with the corn meal mush in the blessing as they had sat down to breakfast, but Sol prayed again. He knew that his father was walking into danger.

Paula stood up and smiled. Sol knew it wasn't a *real* smile, but he was glad to see it anyway.

"Well, we can't sit around here being worried all day. Tonight's Christmas Eve. We've got things to do."

When the molasses on the stove had boiled itself into a sticky mass, it was ready to be made into candy. While it was still warm enough to pull, Sol and Grandma sat at the table and made it into long sticks or into fancy figures. They pulled it into stars, into Santas, into animals. Grandma made a cat with a long tail and even whiskers. And Sol made a horse. And he smiled as he stretched the molasses over the brown paper to make a strong curved back, a neck, legs, head, tail, ears. And with the point of a knife he sculptured into the drying forehead of the animal a small star. Maybe he wouldn't eat this one. Maybe when it was dry, he would hang it up on his window. Probably when the sun came out, it would shine right through it.

"Sol." Paula spoke from the cupboard where she stood loading four baskets with the bread and cookies they had made yesterday. "Grandma and I have got to deliver these baskets. I hate to go today with things so up in the air about the Indians, but I'm afraid if we don't take them, there'll be four families that will have nothing at all for Christmas."

Paula selected a few of the newly-dried candy figures and wrapped them in brown paper. "Why look at that," she said, picking up a little puppy dog that Grandma had made. "Isn't that precious? We'll give that to the Thompson's. Their little boy will love it. Would you like to come with us, Sol?"

"Can't, Ma. I've got an errand of my own. I'm going over to Mr. Kohler's to tell him I've got twenty dollars saved up and ask him to sell me Star."

"You've got to do that today?"

"Yes, Ma. Tomorrow's Christmas. I can maybe have Star for Christmas!"

Paula sighed. She wouldn't turn out the lights in Sol's eyes for anything. "Come on, then. Let's go together as far as Kohler's place."

Sol waved his mother and Grandma on in the wagon and then turned his horse in to Kohler's yard. He heard Star whinnying in the barn. She knows I'm here, Sol thought. Often when Sol came over, Star seemed to be expecting him, looking for him.

The little porch of the farmhouse creaked as Sol stepped up to knock. Mrs. Kohler's face appeared at the window, as a hand suspiciously lifted the curtain a little.

After a few moments the door opened, and Mr. Kohler stood looking down at him. Sol hated to be looked down at. He'd be glad when he was as tall as anybody.

"Yeah?"

"I . . . uh . . . Merry Christmas, Mr. Kohler. I . . . brought you something." Sol held out the little basket he had been carrying.

Mr. Kohler looked at him a moment and almost smiled. "Well . . . come on in."

Sol entered the drab little room. There was no Christmas tree up, no signs of the season at all. The place was clean, but the only attempt at decoration was an odd-looking pink tatted doiley that was fastened to the worn back of a stuffed chair. And a framed picture of a scowling man in a dark suit.

"I've got some candy for the children. Are they here?"

Sol heard a giggle and turned to see a skinny little girl of about seven being pushed into the room by a pair of hands that quickly disappeared. The girl squealed and dashed back out of sight.

"Lucinda! Beth! Come on in here," called Mr. Kohler.

Inch by inch, the little girls appeared, holding each other tightly by the hand. Their hair was braided close against their heads, making them look even skinnier than they were, and their dresses were too small and didn't seem to be any color at all anymore. Their eyes widened as Sol held up two sticks of molasses candy.

"For you," said Sol.

The girls did not move.

"Well, don't just stand there like you got no sense," said Mr. Kohler. "Do you want 'em?"

The girls darted to Sol, grabbed the candy from his hands, giggling, and huddled up against their father. Slowly they put the candy to their lips and gave it a lick.

"Say thank you!" The shrill voice came through the wall.

The girls giggled again. "Thank you," they said together, then darted out of the room.

Sol looked at the big man who was eyeing him suspiciously. "Can I . . . can I talk to you, Mr. Kohler?"

"Go ahead."

Sol sat down on the stuffed chair. He hadn't been asked to, but it seemed strange to talk just standing there. Mr. Kohler pulled up a chair and straddled it like you would straddle a horse.

"Yeah?"

"Well . . ." Now that the time had come, Sol wished he'd written it down and memorized it. "You know how I've been working awful hard? And earning money?"

Mr. Kohler did not respond. Sol hesitated, then spoke

rapidly.

"I want to buy Star off you, Mr. Kohler. Pa says she's worth about fifteen dollars, but I know she's a real fine horse so I'm offering you twenty."

Mr. Kohler's face did not change expression, but he leaned forward a little in his chair. "Twenty dollars? You got twenty dollars?"

"I do."

Kohler's slit eyes narrowed, and he pursed his lips. Suddenly Sol was sorry he'd said twenty. Kohler liked to bargain. He should have started at fifteen and then gone up. What if . . .?

But Mr. Kohler was nodding his head. "Twenty dollars. It's a deal."

"Really?" Sol sat up on the edge of the chair, then caught himself before he became too enthusiastic. He had watched deals being made, and it wasn't a good idea to show too much enthusiasm. It was smart to be even a little reluctant.

"Twenty dollars is an awful lot of money for a horse," he said.

Kohler looked at him unspeaking.

Sol stood up. "Well, then. Tomorrow, if that's all right. Tomorrow morning I'll just bring over twenty dollars and get my horse." Sol had to bite his lip not to smile as he said the words. His horse. *His* horse. Mr. Kohler had agreed. Star was as good as his!

Looking back from the doorway at Mr. Kohler, who still sat straddling the chair, Sol said, "And Merry Christmas."

Then he ran. He didn't even stop to talk to Star. Onto the horse and over the road, faster and faster. He could be enthusiastic now. The deal was made. Laughing, he shouted out to the passing fence posts and the trees, "He said yes! He said yes!"

It was impossible to sit and wait. Sol washed the pots that

his mother had left to soak, scrubbed the molasses drippings off the stove, arranged and rearranged the candy animals on the table. When would his mother and Grandma be coming back? He couldn't wait any longer to tell *someone*.

As he pulled back the red and white checked curtain from the window, Sol saw that it was snowing again. He was glad. Snow for Christmas was always nice. Tomorrow he would walk over, unless it turned into a real blizzard. He would walk over all by himself. It would take him about an hour and a half or more, but the walk would be delicious. Sometimes waiting was wonderful—like saving your Christmas candy and putting it in a clear bottle and knowing that any time you can have a piece if you want to, but waiting anyway.

Sol turned away from the window and went to his bed, kneeling down to pull out the box. It was heavy as he lifted it up onto the quilt. Better count it one more time. That was silly, of course. Sol had counted it so many times that he even found himself doing it in his dreams. One . . . two . . . The counting was delicious, too. He felt . . . powerful. Nineteen . . . twenty. There it was. Twenty dollars.

Sol heard a sound from the yard. Good. Grandma and his mother were back. Quickly Sol swept the money into the box, put the lid on, and thrust it back into the darkness under the bed.

Running through the kitchen, Sol opened the door to greet them. "He said yes! I can . . . ."

Sol froze as he found himself looking directly into the face of an Indian. His dark hair was matted and ragged, and he wore a buckskin shirt and pants. Strips of leather were tied around his feet. His face was thin and drawn, and one eye did not seem to work. There was a white film over it, and the color under the film seemed a milky blue. In the Indian's arms was a bundle, wrapped in a large piece of buckskin.

"I sell. You buy." The Indian took a step nearer to Sol.

Sol fought to beat down the fear that rose in him. Indians came to settlers houses all the time to trade or sell things. There was nothing to be afraid of. The best thing to do was to let him in and feed him. Be friendly. That was the best thing to do. Only he sure did wish his mother and Grandma were here. And especially his father. John would know exactly what to do. Well, Sol had seen his father deal with the Indians dozens of times. He ought to know what to do by now.

"Come in," said Sol, opening the door wider.

The Indian followed him into the kitchen and looked around.

"Sit down." Sol pulled out a chair, and the Indian sat down, holding his bundle on his lap.

"Bet you're hungry, huh?" Sol went to the bread box and pulled out two large loaves. "You can take this here loaf with you, and I'll slice this one up for you right now. And how about some milk? We got some potatoes I can fry up if you want."

The Indian had reached over and grabbed the first slice of bread Sol had cut and was hungrily stuffing it in his mouth.

"Guess I won't take time to fry these up," said Sol as he placed a plate of cold boiled potatoes in front of the Indian. The red man reached for one and devoured it in a few bites.

Sol's hand was shaking as he poured a cup of milk, but tried to keep his voice even. "You know Arrowpine? He's our friend."

The Indian did not reply. Sol had always been taught not to speak with his mouth full, but somehow he didn't think the Indian was quiet out of politeness. He obviously was not here for conversation.

After the Indian had eaten as much as he could, Sol wrapped up the rest of the food — bread, potatoes, some bacon, some dried peaches. There. That would make a good Christmas feast for this Indian and his family.

Suddenly the Indian spoke. "Me sell. You buy."

Sol looked at the bundle still on the Indian's lap. Did he have something he wanted to trade? Sol had gotten another jack-knife. Maybe that would interest him.

The Indian began to unwrap the buckskin covering. Suddenly a sound was heard from within, a soft little whine. And then the buckskin fell away to reveal the black head of a little Indian baby. A baby! Sol sucked in a quick breath and stepped back a little. The Indian wanted to sell . . . a baby?

Thoughts whirled around inside Sol's head like snowflakes in a storm. The Indians *did* sell babies. They sold them into slavery to other tribes or to wandering bands of Mexicans. Brigham Young had encouraged his people to take the children in and raise them as their own. But . . . a baby!

Sol looked at the Indian in horror and shook his head. "No! No! Give baby back to its mother!"

Rudely awakened from the warm nighttime inside the buckskin, the infant began to whimper. It couldn't be more than three months old. A little fist found its way to the mouth, and the baby began to suck.

"No! You buy!"

Sol could hardly believe the words that he heard himself speak. "What you want for him?" Quickly he reached into his pocket and brought out his new jack-knife. Then he undid the elk-tooth necklace that Arrowpine had given him.

"Necklace!" he said. "Indian chief necklace. I give you necklace. You give me baby!"

"No. Money! Baby worth much money!"

"No! No! No money! Take baby back to mother!"

Angrily the Indian stood up, and the baby began to cry. With his good eye, the red man looked down at Sol.

"Money!" he screamed.

Furiously, Sol reached for a solution. There was . . . He had . . . No! That money was for . . .

"No money," he said loudly.

Quickly the Indian dropped the buckskin covering on the floor and held the baby up by its feet. He swung it like a cruel boy would swing a stray cat. "Then me kill baby!"

"No!" Sol felt the blood drain from his face. "No!" he shouted.

The Indian stepped toward the stove and with his good eye on the heavy metal top, swung the baby up as one would swing an ax. The baby wailed in innocent terror.

"Wait!" Sol screamed, and his voice echoed the horror in his heart. The Indian would do it! The Indian would dash the little baby's brains out on the metal stove! He was inhuman. He would do that! "Wait! I . . . I have . . . money!"

The Indian let his arm swing down to his side as he turned to see Sol running into the other room. Quickly Sol leaped under his bed, pulled out the little wooden box, and ran back to the kitchen.

"See? I have money!"

Without a word the Indian opened the box with one hand, still holding the baby by its heels with the other. Then he roughly shoved the baby into Sol's arms, and with the wooden box in one hand and the package of food in the other, he opened the door and was gone.

For minutes Sol stood in the middle of the kitchen holding the baby, his eyes fastened on the door. Had this really happened? Had an Indian just left the house . . . taking with him the twenty dollars he had saved to buy Star? Was there really an Indian baby right here in his arms? The baby began to whimper. It was there all right. Sol sank into a chair and felt his arms shaking as he cradled the infant. Black little eyes looked up at him and blinked. On the table was the candy horse he had made. Star! And in his arms was a little Indian baby. His baby. He had bought . . . a baby!

An hour and a half later when Paula and Grandma came home, they opened the kitchen door to see Sol, sitting in the rocking chair, holding in his arms, wrapped in buckskin, a tiny, dark Indian baby. And singing. "Holy infant, so tender and mild. Sleep in heavenly peace. Sleep in heavenly peace."

CHAPTER SEVEN

J ohn McAllister got back early Christmas morning, weary and dirty, from his journey to the Ute encampment. He had not been able to talk to Arrowpine. The area had been filled with Indian braves, painted and obviously ready to go on the warpath, and there had been no way for John to get through to the chief.

He had been amazed to come home to find a new baby in the house. But he told Sol that he was proud of him, that he knew that Sol had done the right thing.

Christmas morning was spent bathing the baby and making some little flannel clothes and diapers for her. It was a girl, and they debated for a long time over an appropriate name. Should it be an Indian name? A white girl's name?

"I know," said Sol, feeding the little creature a thin paste made of flour and milk. She sucked at the spoon and licked her lips for more. "I think we should name her Eve. She came on Christmas Eve, you know."

"True. Eve's a good name," added John.

"Plus," Sol went on, "Eve was the *first*. And this is the first

Indian baby we've taken in."

"And the last, I hope," said Paula, as she stopped in her work to look down at the little wrinkled face. "The uncivilized barbarians, treating their children like animals."

Sol had been thinking about that. He had stayed up late into the night holding the little baby and rocking her by the light of the oil lamp. Injustice fell on children heaviest of all. Indians could strike back at the white man. Women could reason or run away or beg for mercy. But children? The little infant in his lap was totally helpless. A bigger person could do to her anything he chose. The sweet, innocent eyes could open and shut. The hungry little mouth could cry. But she could not protect herself. She was completely at the mercy of others.

Sol had noticed as he was growing up that adults behaved differently toward children than they did toward each other. Sometimes Sol would walk into the store alone, and the storekeeper would either ignore him or tell him sharply not to touch things. And then when Sol's father would come in, the storekeeper was all smiles and just couldn't do enough for him.

Sol studied the round little face of the baby in his lap. Wasn't the Golden Rule long enough to apply to children? Would it ever be?

Grandma reached down and picked the baby up. "Now, come on, Sol. It's my turn to feed this little what-do-you-call-her? Eve?"

"Eve."

"Well, come here now, Eve." Grandma chuckled, and the wrinkles of her face grew soft as he held the baby up to her shoulder, patting its tiny back. "My word! To think that anybody was ever so small as that!"

Eve grew slowly over the next few months and so did better relations with the Indians and a new pile of coins in a new wooden box.

There were some attacks on white settlers up north, a few

deaths reported, and quite a number of cattle stolen. But gradually things settled back down to normal, and the Indians and the white settlers looked at each other with only the usual amount of hostility.

About the time Eve began to smile, Sol erased the hurt he felt every time he remembered that he had traded the baby for Star. She was a bright light in the house, chattering and gooing, and Grandma loved her even more than she loved the rag doll she had gotten for Christmas. They would sit in the rocking chair for hours—Grandma with her alive little brown doll and her quiet little pink and white rag doll, all three of them looking like they belonged on the shelf of a store at Christmas time.

Mr. Kohler had laughed long and loud when he learned that Sol had spent his twenty dollars on an Injun baby. But he agreed that when the boy earned up another twenty dollars, he could have Star. There wasn't much work in the winter, though, and Sol knew it would probably be summer before he could count on having that much money. In the meantime he fed Star, brushed her, talked to her. He spent a long time trying to explain to her about the baby. Star nuzzled him warmly, and Sol knew she understood. Mr. Kohler didn't—he had told Sol outright that he was a fool. But Star understood—she knew Sol had done the right thing.

"I'll bring Eve over to see you sometime, Star. When she gets a little bigger. She'd like that. You'd like to see her, too, huh? Wouldn't you, Star?"

One afternoon in May, as Sol was coming back in to Mr. Kohler's yard from planting potatoes, he saw Kohler leading Star from the barn out to a corral. Sol followed them.

"It's about time this here filly got broke," Kohler said. The long piece of grass he held in his teeth moved up and down like an orchestra conductor's baton as he spoke. "Reckon she's gettin' close to two years now. Time to break her—make her useful."

"You mean . . . today?" Sol's eyes brightened.

"Yup. Right now."

"Can I watch?"

"Won't stop ya."

Star's ears were laid back against her head, and Sol noticed a wild look in her eyes. Star didn't like Mr. Kohler. Sol knew that. She always acted different when he was around. When they were alone, she was calm and happy and loving.

He'd never have said that to Mr. Kohler, of course. He'd laugh even louder than he had when he learned Sol had bought the Indian baby. But Star *was* loving. At least she was to Sol.

"Hey, now! Don't get uppity with me, you hear?" Kohler jerked the halter, and Star reluctantly moved closer to the fence, where he tied her securely. Her feet were dancing nervously, and her whinny betrayed an unrest.

"I'll just put this here saddle on first," said Kohler, as he reached for the dark leather saddle that was straddling the fence. "Got to get an animal used to having something on its back before you climb on. Whoa, now!"

Sol climbed up onto the fence so he could see the whole show.

"After she's broke—can I ride her?" The very thought of being able to climb onto Star's back and taking off over the fields made his heart leap.

Kohler grinned. His grin was never a smile. It always jumped over being a smile and landed on being a mocking sort of expression, like he found you very amusing and foolish. But Sol didn't care this time. Soon he could ride Star!

The saddle landed deftly on Star's back, and she reared up on her back legs with a sharp whinny, throwing the saddle askew. Mr. Kohler pulled the saddle down and positioned it again for the throw.

"Damn horse has to know who's boss. Now, hold still!"

Again Mr. Kohler threw the saddle, and again Star reared, this time pawing the air with her front feet and whinnying wildly.

Sol wanted to say, "Let me put it on. She'd let me do it.

She doesn't *like* you, Mr. Kohler." But he couldn't say that. So he just sat on the fence and hung on tight to a pole as if he might be thrown off.

Kohler had stepped back from Star and was looking at her through the hard slits of his eyes. "So," he drawled. "You want to fight, huh?" Then he lifted a leather whip, raised it, and cracked it across Star's smooth, black back. Sol and Star cried out together, their voices blending in pain.

"No!" called Sol. "Don't!"

"Take it easy, kid," Mr. Kohler said with his hateful grin. "Just showin' her who's boss. You got to show 'em who's boss."

Star danced in the dust, her neck tugging against the leather strap that held her to the fence. And for a moment her wild, black eyes reminded him of the eyes of the Indian baby on Christmas Eve.

Kohler picked up the saddle again and threw it onto the filly's back. Star lunged to one side with an angry snort, and white teeth flashed as she nipped at Mr. Kohler's arm. Kohler yelped and drew back. His sleeve was ripped, and a little line of red showed through the cloth.

"Damn son of a ---." Kohler's face was suddenly aflame with rage, and he lunged for the whip on the ground.

"No! Don't!" Sol drew his legs up under him on the top log of the fence and dug his fingernails into his knees. "Don't whip her!"

"Shut up, kid. No damn horse is gonna put her teeth into me!"

Then he raised the whip, and Sol winced as it cracked and landed on Star's back. The filly screamed and reared and pulled violently against the leather strap. Again the whip went up, and again it came down on the quivering black flesh of the animal.

"No!" screamed Sol. "No!"

There was something primitive in Kohler's eyes as his arm rose and fell, something dark and ugly that went back untold centuries — back as far as the first violence ever done by man to another living being. His eyes were filled with the need to triumph, the need to stand victor, the ancient, ancient need to show who's boss.

Sol leapt to his feet on the top log of the fence and looked down as the whip left its mark in the black flesh, like ice skates left marks on a frozen lake. Only these marks were . . . red! Star was bleeding!

"Stop!" Sol screamed. "You coward! Beating a helpless animal! She's bleeding! Stop!"

"Shut up!" Kohler snarled and lifted the whip again.

"She's got more soul than you do!" Sol sobbed and screamed at the same time. "And so do the Indians! It's you that maybe has no soul, Mr. Kohler, and if you do, you'll probably go straight to hell! Stop it!"

His words seemed to fuel Kohler's anger even more, for the whipping continued. The filly screamed, and the boy sobbed, both helpless, helpless as one is always helpless who is not boss.

And then, without consciously deciding to, Sol hurled himself from the log fence, hurled himself onto the big man with the whip. The two of them hit the ground together and rolled over in the dust of the corral. Sol grabbed for the whip, but Kohler held it firm and leapt to his feet, giving Sol a mighty kick that sent him smashing into the wooden fence.

Sol looked up to see Mr. Kohler standing over him, breathing hard, his face as red as smoking coals, and his whip arm raised. Sol closed his eyes and steeled himself for the crash of the whip. But it didn't come. Slowly he opened his eyes. Kohler stood above him, arms at his sides, the whip coiled in the dust like a snake.

"You get off my property," he said slowly, eyes boring into Sol like hot pokers. "You get off and stay off. I don't never want to see you on this place again. I wouldn't sell you this here horse for five hundred dollars, you hear? You'll never see her again! Now, get!"

Sol stumbled to his feet and looked through blinding tears at Star, pawing the ground and moaning deep in her throat.

And then he ran.

When Sol got home, he didn't go in the house right away. He put the horse in the barn and then, almost without thinking about it, crawled into the wheat bin. It was like a small room filled three or four feet high with wheat. Sol had always liked to come out here to play in the golden grain. But today he came just to be alone, maybe like animals go alone somewhere to lick their wounds.

He dug himself deep into the wheat, covering his legs, his body, his arms and hands. Only his head was free, lying back on a pillow of wheat. Gradually he stopped sobbing and just lay there, quiet. He was beyond putting his pain into words. He just lay there and let his pain course through him. And he let the cooling wheat draw it out, draw out the poison pain and plant in him a little comfort, a little peace. For more than an hour he lay in the wheat, staring at the small spot in the roof that let in the sky.

Sol sat between his father and mother on the little couch. His father's arm was around his shoulders, and his mother's hand tried to smooth the fist that would not be smoothed.

"He just stood there, beating her and beating her." Telling the story made the tears come again. "I couldn't help myself. And now, I'll never see . . ." He broke off and slammed a fist into his palm. "I hate him! I hate him! I hate him!"

"I understand, son. I understand." His father spoke quietly. Having seen injustice for three times as many years as his son had, he was more used to it. But to see it come this close to one he loved was hard.

Paula pressed her son's hand to her cheek. It used to be easy to heal Sol's hurts. A song and a joke could do it. But the world had a way of giving out hurts that got harder and harder to heal.

"I know this won't help much, son," said John after a few moments. "But I want to tell you about Nat Kohler."

"I hate him!"

"I know you do, son. But it helps a little bit when you can see behind what a person does. Nat Kohler was born in Missouri . . ."

"How do you know?"

"Bishop Watts knew the family back there. He thought it might help me to understand my neighbor, so he told me. Kohler's mother died when he was a baby, and he was raised— if you can call it that—by a drunkard father. The father would beat him anytime he took a mind to. Near killed him a time or two. When young Nat was about seven or eight, he got mean and rebellious. You can understand why. His father thought he was losing control over him, so he worked out a plan with his brother, Nat's uncle, to scare the living daylights out of the boy."

"What plan?" It had never really occurred to Sol that Nat Kohler was ever a little boy.

"Well, Nat's father told him that if he ever disobeyed again, he was going to take him down to the river and drown him. So the next time Nat disobeyed, his father took him down to the river and put him in the water and held him there. Nat's uncle was there behind a tree, just like they had planned, and after the boy was under water for a minute or two, he came over and pushed Nat's father to the ground and pulled the boy out of the water. The two men fought for a minute—all planned out, of course, and finally Nat's father agreed that he would let the boy go this time, but that if he ever disobeyed again, it was the end."

Sol was aghast. Nat's father would let the boy think he would actually *drown* him?

"So up until Nat's father died in a brawl in a saloon, Nat lived in terror of him. Can you imagine what that would do to the inside of somebody—to believe that your father would drown you? Might make you pretty mean."

Sol sighed. Why did things get so complicated? It was easier to hate somebody when you didn't feel sorry for him at the same time. Nat Kohler beat Star. Nat's father beat him. And did the father's father beat him, too? Does it go on and on like the ripples in a pond when you throw a pebble in? But it has to stop somewhere. You can't just be mean because somebody else was mean to you. Somewhere it has to stop. Someone has to say no.

It was close to midnight when Sol snuck out of the house. In his hands were Grandma's bottle of mineral water and one of Eve's little flannel diapers. A full moon lit his walk down the road and through the fields. It smelled like spring. The earth didn't give up, and Sol was glad. Every year, no matter how hard and cold the winter had been, she tried again, and pretty soon green things came up.

There was no sound but the crickets as Sol softly crept into the barn toward the stalls. He left the door open a little so enough moon would get in for him to see by. The shaft of light fell directly on Star's stall. Sol crept closer and stuck his head through the narrow logs. There she was—lying down on some hay. Sol had never seen her lying down before. She had always been standing, nose thrust through the stall, waiting for him and whinnying.

"Hi, Star," Sol whispered. "Hi, girl."

The animal lifted its head, and a sound came out—not a whinny—almost a moan. Sol threw himself down on the hay beside her, and again he felt the tears warm his eyes. His arms went around the filly's neck, and he buried his face in her mane.

"I'm sorry, Star. I'm sorry," he murmured.

Sol twisted the lid from Grandma's bottle of mineral water and poured some onto the flannel diaper.

"I hope this doesn't hurt, Star. But it'll do you good. You'll see."

Gently the boy touched the damp cloth to the welts on the filly's back. He could see them even by the pale light of the moon that flooded in the barn door. Star shuddered and moved as if she would stand up. "No, Star. No. This will help. You know I love you. You know I wouldn't do anything to you that wouldn't be good. Trust me, Star. Just trust me."

The filly nuzzled her nose into Sol's chest, and Sol put his lips on the white star on her forehead. Then he poured a little more mineral water on the cloth, and gently—very gently— touched it again to Star's back. Star shuddered and was still.

"I *will* see you again, Star," Sol whispered. "I'll never desert you. I promise."

When Sol stole out of the barn and shut the door behind him, he reckoned it was about four o'clock. He didn't dare risk staying until dawn. Soon he'd tell Grandma what had happened to all of her mineral water. He wouldn't lie to an Indian, and he wouldn't lie to Grandma. She would understand.

CHAPTER EIGHT

Barn-raisings were fun. Sol loved to see something as big as a barn go into place all in one day. Settlers from miles around had come to raise a barn for the Cummings family. Sol had turned thirteen last month in June and was considered one of the men now. He stood with them shoulder to shoulder lifting the logs in place and watching the walls get higher and higher. As soon as the roof was on, they were going to celebrate with supper out here in the yard, and then all go inside for a barn dance. Brother Stewart had brought his fiddle, Brother Spencer had brought his accordian, and Sol was sure a guitar or banjo would show up, too.

Sol liked the dances. There weren't any girls around that were worth looking at, but he loved the music. They'd probably dance the quadrille, the Virginia reel, and the money musk. Lining up and stomping and bowing — that was fun. That was enough to make Sol forget — for a little while anyway — that life was pretty grim . . . that real peace with the Indians was still quite a ways down the road and that once in a while in the middle of the night was the only time he could ever see Star.

He had seen Kohler riding her a couple of times, so he figured she was broke. Sol wished he'd ridden her over to the barn-raising, but Star wasn't here, and Kohler wasn't here either. He had gotten more and more anti-social it seemed, and if there was a place where a group of Mormons would be, that's where he'd stay away from.

After the barn was finished, the children went to play while the women finished making supper and the men set up the tables. Sol went with the children. It was sometimes convenient to be right in the middle of being a boy and a man, and he could go either way he chose. And right now he chose to be a boy.

Down at the creek was a large swing between two trees. It swung right over the water, and the young people delighted in seeing how close they could come to touching the water without really getting wet. Then they played steal the stick, run sheep run, and pitched horseshoes.

By the time supper was called, Sol was ready. He sat at a table with his family, bouncing Eve on his knee and feeding her bits from his own plate. Everybody knew the baby belonged to him. And nobody but Kohler had laughed about it. Everybody else had made a hero out of him. It had gotten around real fast that Sol had saved the baby's life. The bishop had even used it as an example of true Christian service in a church meeting.

They were finishing supper when the musicians began setting up. Jenkins Broadhead stood and pounded on the table for attention.

"Well, we're going to have a little singing here while we're waiting for the melons and the pies. But first off I got a little story to tell you."

A few groans were heard. Jenkins was famous for his little stories, and especially for the fact that he laughed like it was the first time he'd ever heard them.

"Well, I heard this conversation while I was over visiting young Nicholas Parry and his wife the other day. 'Nicholas,' says Martha. 'I wish you would rock the baby.' 'Why, what'll I rock the baby for?' asks Nicholas. 'Because he's not very well,' says Martha. 'And what's more, half of him belongs to you, and you should not object to rocking him.' And then says Nicholas, 'Well, don't half belong to you?' 'Yes,' says Martha. 'Well, you can rock your half,' says Nicholas, 'and let my half holler.'"

Jenkins held his sides and laughed. Others laughed, too, and Sol even smiled. Grandma chuckled, making Eve's little black head bob up and down on her shoulder.

"We're going to . . ." Jenkins was still catching his breath from such a good laugh. "We're going to sing now. What'll be first?" Hands shot up, and a few people called out favorites. "Now, before we leave off, we'll get around to every song that anybody here wants to sing, but what'll it be to begin with?"

Two small children jumped up and down and called out, "Whoa, Haw, Buck and Jerry Boy!"

Jenkins smiled. "Sounds like a good one to me! You ready on the fiddle?"

Jenkins turned to Brother Stewart who nodded and lifted the bow.

"And how about that there accordian, Brother Spencer? Can that still roll over your stomach, or will it pinch some of those good sweet potatoes I saw you gobbling down?"

Brother Spencer waved him away and sounded a chord. Nobody needed to lead the singing. These folks were used to just joining in like they just joined in to raise a barn.

"With a merry little jig and a gay little song,
Whoa, Haw, Buck, and Jerry Boy,
We trudge our way the whole day long,
Whoa, Haw, Buck, and Jerry Boy.
What though we're covered all over with dust?
It's better than staying back home to rust.
We'll reach Salt Lake some day or bust.
Whoa, Haw, Buck, and Jerry Boy."

Sol sang enthusiastically, clapping Eve's little hands together to the rhythm of the music. This was one of the songs that had cheered them as they made their way across the great plains to the Salt Lake Valley. At night they would bring their wagons around in a ring for better protection against Indians and animals. And then they would sing and dance. Even when they didn't feel like it, they would sing and dance, and before long they would feel like it. This was one of Sol's favorites.

"There's a pretty little girl in the outfit ahead,
Whoa, Haw, Buck, and Jerry Boy.
I wish she was by my side instead,
Whoa, Haw, Buck, and Jerry Boy.
Look at her now with a pout on her lips
As daintily with her fingertips
She picks for the fire some buffalo chips,
Whoa, Haw, Buck, and Jerry Boy."

The accordian player was just getting set to pump out the last verse when Sol noticed some riders on horses coming down the road fast. They stopped behind the new barn, and one of the men hurried over to Bishop Watts and spoke quietly in his ear. The bishop got up and hurried behind the barn. The messenger then spoke to two other men and to John McAllister, who also got up and left the singing.

"What is it, Pa?"

But John did not stop to reply. Sol handed Eve to Grandma and followed the men. If something was going on, he wanted to know. He stood beside the fence and listened. The men were too involved to notice him anyway.

"You certain it was Kohler?" the Bishop was asking.

"Course I'm certain," panted the rider. "I saw him raise his gun myself, and I saw him fire. We were near the lake, and this here Indian was hunting game with bows and arrows. Kohler comes along and tells him to clear off because he plans to homestead ten acres right there. The Indian says no, the white men promised to leave this land to them. Kohler says to get off, or he'll shoot. The Indian starts to raise his bow, and Kohler aims his gun. And he fires."

The man turned toward his horse, and for the first time

Sol noticed the large bulge behind the saddle. With a quick motion, the man pulled off from the horse a plain gray blanket, revealing the body of an Indian tied over the horse with ropes. He wasn't very big—probably not even a full grown man. Around his neck was a . . . Sol stepped closer. Was it? An elk-tooth necklace like his and like the one he had seen on Arrowpine's son. Was this . . . ? The picture of an Indian boy pleading with his father to let his sister go flashed into Sol's memory. This was the same face. It was!

"What do we do with him?" asked Jenkins Broadhead.

"Bury him," said another man who had ridden in. "I told him that. Bury him, and maybe the tribe will never know. They'll think maybe animals got him."

Bishop Watts thought a moment. "That's not right," he said. "We can't do that."

"There were probably other Indians nearby anyway," added Jenkins. "They keep track of each other. They know."

"But maybe they won't," argued the man. "If hiding him would avoid trouble, we ought to try it. If there's a chance that they won't miss him . . ."

"They'll miss him," Sol interrupted, taking a step closer to the men.

The men turned to look at Sol.

"How do you know, son?" asked John.

"Pa," Sol gestured to the dead Indian on the horse, "that Indian is Arrowpine's son."

John McAllister looked as though he had suddenly been punched in the stomach and slowly turned to the dead Indian.

"I know it is, Pa," continued Sol. "I saw him when I went with Arrowpine last summer. See? He has a necklace exactly like the one the chief gave me!"

"Oh, no," said Bishop Watts, putting a hand to his forehead. "Oh, no!"

"Blast that Nat Kohler!" exclaimed the rider.

The men were silent for a moment, each of them envisioning the reprisals that were sure to follow. Arrowpine had refused to meet with the other Indian chiefs and the white men to pow-wow and try again for peace. And now to have his son killed could mean all-out war.

"Put the boy on my horse," ordered John.

"What?"

"I'm taking him to his father. And I will plead with Arrowpine to meet with us one more time to work out terms of peace."

"John . . . you're crazy," said Jenkins. "Arrowpine won't listen."

"Maybe not. But if he'll listen to anybody, he'll listen to me."

"It's a wild chance, John," said the bishop anxiously. "We don't want to lose you."

"I know it's only a chance. But it's a chance I've got to take. Without it, I'm afraid we're in for all-out war. Sol, go get your mother."

Sol knew better than to question his father when he saw a certain determined look on his face. And that look was there now. Quickly he went back to the tables.

In a matter of minutes the body of Arrowpine's son was transferred to John's horse. John said goodbye to his wife and mother and son. The bishop and Jenkins Broadhead gave him a special blessing, laying their hands on his head, and John rode off, a pole secured to his saddle, from which waved the white flag of a shirt.

The bishop made a general announcement for all to go directly home as quickly as possible and exercise more than usual caution, for there had been some trouble with the Indians. But he didn't tell them exactly what the trouble was. No use causing panic if it wasn't necessary.

The silence of the ride home was broken only by Paula's occasional exclamation, "Why does it always have to be *him*?"

And again neither Sol nor Grandma answered the question

because they knew it wasn't really a question. And Sol knew too that in spite of the terror she felt about her husband riding alone into Indian territory, she was proud of him. Very proud. He was a man of enormous courage, and Paula wouldn't have it any other way.

They arrived home well before dark and went about their evening chores. Grandma busied herself with Eve, heating the water for her bath, gently washing the fattening little body, and dressing her in a clean flannel nightgown.

Together Sol and his mother went out to milk the cows. It would not do to leave cows unmilked, except for an actual emergency, which they did not feel this was—not yet. Unmilked cows would moo out their pain all night.

As Sol arranged the stool by the cow's heavy bag, he heard the quick darts of milk hit the metal pail as his mother, only a few feet away, began milking Daisy. Sol remembered how his father had joked about her milking. He wished his father were here now to make a few jokes. Maybe he would have to try to come up with one himself. Sol milked for a while and thought, but nothing came except the thin, white streams that burst into foam as they hit the warm liquid in the bottom of the bucket.

They had been working for about five minutes when Sol suddenly noticed that his mother's hands were still.

"Shhhhh," she said.

Sol stopped his milking and listened. Only the moo of one of the cows could be heard. And then—the unmistakable yelp that they knew by now meant Indians. And the pounding of the horses' hoofs on the road.

"Quickly!" Paula jumped to her feet and ran to the door of the barn, followed closely by Sol. They peered out and saw, perhaps a quarter of a mile down the road, a band of Indians, painted for war. Their leader, in a long feathered headdress that reached to the belly of his spotted Appaloosa, raised his arm, and the band behind him slowed their horses. There were perhaps twenty warriors, each with bows and arrows slung over their shoulders and several carrying guns.

"Run!" Paula threw herself out the barn door, picked up her skirts, and ran as fast as she could for the house, followed closely by Sol. If the Indians saw them, they did not break the slow rhythm of their approach. Sol and Paula hurled themselves into the house and bolted the door behind them.

"Indians, Grandma! It's Indians!" cried Sol. "Pa was too late. They're already on the warpath!"

"I don't think so," said Paula, standing beside the window and carefully peering out. "I don't believe these are Utes at all. I think they're Shoshonis."

"Shoshonis!" echoed Sol. He ran to the window and joined his mother. Was that any comfort? Shoshonis had a reputation for being even more blood-thirsty than the Utes.

"Look!" cried Paula. "They're coming right into the yard!"

Three pair of eyes watched from the window as the Indians tied up their horses and began building a fire.

"They're setting up camp," said Sol. "Ma, look . . . they're setting up camp!"

"Here?" Grandma put her hand on Paula's shoulder and held on tight.

"What do you suppose they want, Ma?" Sol was almost afraid to voice the question.

"I . . . I don't know." Paula forced a calmness into her voice and went on. "It could be that this is a war party out after some Utes. The Shoshonis and the Utes are bitter enemies, you know. And seeing our well here, they decided this would make a good place to spend the night. Yes, I think that seeing our well, they decided to make camp here."

That could be it, thought Sol. But he knew there were other possibilities, too. He knew that they could be on a general rampage, killing whatever white men happened across their path. He knew that any minute now — or in the middle of the night — the Indians could break in and massacre all of them. That, he thought, would be just as likely.

The minutes went by slowly as they watched the Indians. Would they come up to the house? Would they ask for food? But they cooked something over their campfire, got water from the well, and ignored the farmhouse.

After a while Paula left the window and sat down in the chair, leaning her head back and closing her eyes. "I think they're not going to bother us," she said. "I think they just needed a campground. Come on, Grandma, let's get ready for bed."

In a few minutes, all three, dressed in their night clothes, sat down in the kitchen for their evening reading of the Bible. They were in Psalms now. They read about fifteen minutes every night.

"'The Lord is my light and my salvation. Who shall I fear?'" Paula read in a strong and even voice. "'The Lord is the strength of my life. Of whom shall I be afraid!'"

She stopped reading abruptly and looked at Sol, who was looking at her. What was that sound? A drum! The tapping of a drum came from the Indian camp. A war whoop! And then another!

Grandma sat still with her hands pressed against her heart, and Sol moved quietly to the window. Outside in the yard the braves were dancing. *Why were they dancing? Why the war whoops? Why the drum?* Didn't they only do that when . . . ? When they were about to . . . ?

"What shall we do, Ma?"

"I don't know, Sol. I don't know."

"There's . . . there's the gun."

Paula shook her head. Then she walked over to Grandma, who was rocking back and forth, holding her head in her hands. She knelt down and kissed the wrinkled cheek. "Well, that's all the scripture reading for tonight, Grandma. Time for prayer."

They knelt together on the hard floor of the kitchen. Paula closed her eyes and bowed her head. Sol and Grandma followed.

"Dear Heavenly Father. Thank you for our lives and for all good things. We need your help tonight. Please keep us safe from the Indians and show us what to do. And bless John the same. In Jesus' name, amen."

Paula didn't get up for a minute. She just knelt there with her eyes closed as if listening. Then she stood up and spoke firmly. "Grandma . . . Sol . . . I want you to go get the blankets from your beds and follow me."

"Wha . . . ?"

"Just do as I say, please."

In a moment they all stood in the kitchen with their blankets and pillows. Paula reached into Eve's little basket and picked up the sleeping baby. She secured the blankets around her and handed the child to Sol.

"Now, follow me."

"Paula . . ." Grandma's voice quavered.

"It's all right, Grandma. Just follow me."

Paula unbarred the kitchen door, opened it, and stepped out. Sol followed with Eve and behind him came Grandma. The tapping of the drum stopped. The warriors stopped dancing. All the Indians watched in absolute stillness as two white women in nightgowns and a white boy with a baby walked out of the house and directly into their camp.

Paula approached the Indian in the long headdress. Red and blue stripes on his brown skin shone in the light of the fire. His dark eyes stared in surprise as the white women stopped before him.

"You chief?" asked Paula.

"Me chief," answered the Indian.

"What's your name?"

"Name Running Fox."

Paula nodded. "Running Fox great chief. Running Fox good, brave chief. We fear Utes. Utes kill white man. Utes maybe come tonight. We are glad to see Running Fox. Running Fox protect us from the Utes. Here with great chief Running Fox we are safe."

Sol listened open-mouthed to his mother. She was . . . putting the Shoshoni chief in charge of protecting them!

"Put your blanket down right here, Sol. Grandma, you put yours right here."

The three white people arranged their blankets on the ground, lay down on them, and pulled other blankets over them. Eve was cradled in Sol's arm.

"Well, good night, Grandma," said Paula cheerfully. "Good night, Sol. Good night, Chief Running Fox."

Paula closed her eyes. Sol closed his, too. But he peeked out through one eyelid just enough to see the Shoshoni chief motion six of his braves to take positions at various places around the fire. Good, brave chief Running Fox would protect them. Sol put his forehead down onto Eve's warm little cheek and slept.

CHAPTER NINE

John McAllister was used to walking into surprises when he came back from being gone. Still he was startled to ride into his farmyard and see twenty or so Shoshoni braves camped out and eating breakfast, served by his family. They were wolfing down cornbread, bacon, milk, and grunting for more.

While Paula said good-bye to the Indians and thanked Chief Running Fox again for protecting them, Sol told his father the events of the night before and how Paula had made them walk right into the Indian camp.

"She looked right at the Shoshoni chief and told him he had to protect us from the bad Indians. You'd have been proud of her, Pa."

"I am, son," said John, putting his arms around Paula, who had just come in the door. "I'm very proud of her."

"It wasn't my idea," said Paula. "It was given to me. A voice spoke in my head and said, 'This is what you must do.' So I did it."

"Did you find Arrowpine, Pa?"

John sat down wearily and ran his fingers through his dusty hair. "I did."

"What did he say?"

"He said he will no more talk peace with the white man. He said every treaty the white man made with him has been broken. He says the white men are without honor—that I am the only honest white man there is."

"So he will not come to the pow-wow," said Paula sadly.

"Never. All the other chiefs have agreed. I think that this time we could make some real progress toward peace. But without Arrowpine there, the pow-wow will mean nothing."

"And what about . . . his son?" Sol felt a wave of fear even as he asked the question.

John heaved a sigh and then stood up, drawing both his wife and his son into his arms. "Other braves were not far off. They know who shot him. Arrowpine has said that Nat Kohler must be turned over to the tribe by noon today—or there will be war, and they will kill every white man they can find in the entire territory."

Sol pulled back a little and looked up into his father's face. "We'll do it—won't we?"

"Give them Kohler?" John slowly shook his head. "We can't." He crossed the window, looked out, and then turned to face them. "We just can't."

"Why not?" asked Sol. "He did it. Kohler shot him. He deserves to be punished."

"Tortured to death? Killed in the most inhuman way? We can't turn a man over to a fate like that. Civilized people don't do it. I'm not too fond of Nat Kohler, but I could never live with myself turning him over to the Indians."

"So what are we going to do?" Paula's eyes were filled with fear. It was exhausting to have fear come and go and then come again so quickly like waves on a shore. "That gives us only about five hours."

"We're heading for the fort—everybody is. I talked with the bishop and other men early this morning. They all agreed. Riders are out alerting everybody to gather a few things fast and go to the fort. It'll take us about an hour to get there. Where's Grandma?"

"She's lying down. Last night was hard on her. Let's not wake her 'til it's time to go." Paula quickly began putting food and dishes into the baskets.

"Help your ma load up the wagon, son," said John. "I'll be getting the livestock ready."

"Pa, what about the animals out in the far pasture?"

"We'll probably never see them again, son. There's no way we can get to them in time. I expect the Indians to come through and round up every living thing they see." John moved to the door. "Put in enough supplies for a month anyway. We've sent for the militia, but I'm afraid it'll take more than soldiers for Arrowpine to change his mind."

Paula drove the wagon, and Grandma held the baby. Sol and John were in front of them herding the livestock. Cows and horses and a few sheep voiced their objections to being hurried along the road. A few of the best laying hens were crated up in the wagon, but most of the poultry had to be left behind.

They passed Kohler's place and waved at the bishop, who was there helping load the wagon. Sol almost smiled as he saw Kohler coming out of the house with a large sack of potatoes. He'd never seen the man move that fast before!

As they approached the fort, they became one of the many groups that were pouring into the open doors of the large structure. Its high wooden walls had been built by the settlers as their first project in the valley. They had lived inside those protecting walls for their first year here. And when they had left, Sol had hoped that they'd left for good. But it looked like a good place to come to now. The wide open doors were safe, welcoming arms.

Inside, all was confusion. A man stood on a wagon, directing families to different sections of the fort, and pointing the way to take the animals. The bellowing of cows and the crying of babies and voices calling for information or giving it — all combined into a stream of sound that rolled on and on.

When they had stopped the wagon beside the small shed that was to be their home, and herded their cattle in with the others, Sol ran to peek through the nearest rifle hole. Wagons were still arriving. Could they all fit in the fort? But he knew they could. The fort had taken a long time to build, and it was huge. Sol remembered carrying the fifteen-foot logs, split in two, and raising them, bark side to the outside and smooth split side to the inside. All the reinforcing was done on the inside, of course. No one on the outside could get a toe-hold if he tried to climb up the slick bark. And on opposite sides of the fort were two lookout towers. Men would soon be up there and would stay there, rifles in hand, as long as the settlers had to remain in the fort.

Sol peeked out again through the rifle hole. In only a few hours, would war-painted Indians appear on the horizon? It was exciting. Sol did not *want* the Indians to come. He did not *want* the settlers to have to be in the fort. He did not *want* Kohler to have killed Arrowpine's son. But as long as all of it was happening, he might as well enjoy the excitement of it.

Sol helped his mother and Grandma organize their little camp, and then he went off by himself to look around. His father was over by the livestock, helping to arrange the feeding and watering. Maybe Sol would go on over and have a good visit with Star. He hadn't seen her in the daylight for a long time, and Kohler would not be able to object to him seeing her. Kohler was not in a position to object to anything.

Moving quickly through the wagons and the tents that were going up, Sol was suddenly grateful for this whole adventure. Grandma had always told him that if you look hard enough, you can find the good in anything. And Sol had found it today without having to look very hard at all. For as long as they had to stay in the fort, he could go and spend time with Star, as much time as he wanted.

Sol stopped as he saw — a little ways apart from everybody else — Nat Kohler and his family, sitting quietly in their wagon, looking around as if they didn't quite know what had happened to them. Everybody else was hustling about, but Nat Kohler just sat on his wagon, staring at his hands that still held the reins of his horses. Mrs. Kohler had a fearful look on her pinched face, and once in a while her elbows went out and then back in under her shawl, as if she was a dark little bird attempting to fly away. The two small girls sat close to each other in the back of the wagon, pulling their thin dresses down over their knees and rounding their shoulders in as if to become smaller and smaller.

What was Nat Kohler thinking, Sol wondered. Nobody seemed to be paying any attention to him, but the extra wide spaces that had been left on either side of his wagon indicated that maybe nobody wanted to be close neighbors with him. Everyone knew that he was the reason they were all here. Was Kohler surprised that the settlers had refused to hand him over to the Indians? Was he grateful? Or was gratitude even one of the feelings he had stocked up on the shelves inside? Sol had not seen evidence of any feelings but the hard ones. Maybe sometime while they were here, Sol would go speak to him, say something to cheer him up. After all, loving your enemies was something he had been taught over and over again in church. Maybe later on he would try it.

But right now he was in too much of a hurry to see Star. He ran through the dust and jumped over wagon tongues and darted around small children. There were the animals — all together in a mooing, whinnying, bleating mass. Good thing all the animals were branded. It would be impossible ever to get them in the right piles after this kind of shuffling.

Of course, he wouldn't have to look for the "K" on Star's hind quarters to recognize her. He'd hated even to look at Kohler's brand on her hide, and he used to plan how he could change the brand into some other symbol once Star was his. But he hadn't done much thinking about that lately.

There was a "K" on a horse! And another one. And on a few cows. Star would not be far away. Sol walked through the moving herds, eyes searching for the familiar white star on the black forehead. There were some of his father's animals with the bar-M clearly identifying them. Sol emerged from the herd on the other side, looking around puzzled. How had he missed Star? She was here—wasn't she?

Something unwelcome as winter and just as cold crept into his stomach as Sol faced the thought. Star hadn't been left—out there somewhere, had she? He ran through the herd again, turning his head madly from left to right, reading the animals as if they were words on a page and the story just had to come out all right. It had to!

But Star was nowhere to be seen. Maybe . . . Sol dashed to the nearest lookout tower and climbed frantically up and up. Maybe up here he could see her. Maybe she was just hidden somehow.

Sol studied the herds. There were plenty of black horses, but none of them was Star. Wait! That one had a white foot— and another white foot! But her head faced the other way. Maybe . . . She turned, and her solid black head made Sol moan aloud in disappointment.

Hurriedly he climbed partway down the tower and leapt the last ten feet. He'd go ask Mr. Kohler. He didn't want to, but he had to. He *had* to *know*!

Sol raced back to where Kohler was now unloading his wagon.

"Mr. Kohler," he panted. "Where's Star?"

Kohler looked up, a bushel of corn in his arms, pressed against his belly. "Huh?"

"Star . . . she's here, isn't she? She's safe, isn't she?"

"She ain't here." Kohler turned to take the corn into the shed.

Sol ran and stood in front of him and looked directly into his eyes. "Where *is* she?"

"Out in the north forty. Last week, took about a dozen

horses out there to pasture. Had to leave 'em." Kohler brushed past Sol and disappeared into the shed.

Star was . . . not here! The fact slowly settled in Sol's mind like a bucket that lowers into a well and fills with water. In a few hours or a day the Indians would ride through and gather every animal in sight. Star would be taken to the Ute encampment. And then she would probably be traded to another tribe, maybe taken to California! He would never see her again. He would never see Star again!

Sol didn't really plan what he did next. He just did it. It wasn't like making up the story as you go along. It was like turning the page, and the story is already written and you just read it.

Sol ran back to his family's camp. No one was there. Quickly Sol rummaged through the boxes that had been brought in from the wagon. Somewhere there would be that little cigar box. Pa had never smoked a cigar, but someone had given him the little box, and he kept all his important papers in it. There were always pencils in it, too.

Sol found it without too much trouble and opened it. He took out a pencil, and after a quick search found a blank piece of paper.

"Dear Pa and Ma and Grandma, I have gone out to bring in Star. She was left like we left some of our horses, and I have got to go get her. I promised Star that I would never let her be taken away. I promised her I would keep her safe. I hope you will understand and . . ."

Sol frowned as he stared at the paper. They wouldn't understand. His father would organize a party to go out and bring him back. And then maybe they would *all* be killed by Indians. If death was the price Sol had to pay for trying to rescue Star, then that's the price he had to pay. But he couldn't let his father and other men risk their lives, too. Quickly Sol tore up the paper into tiny pieces and hid them in his pocket. Then he found another piece of blank paper and scribbled a quick message.

"I am all right. Do not worry about me. I'll be back soon." There. They wouldn't know where to look now. And until nightfall they would assume he was somewhere in the fort. Sol put the note where it would easily be found, put the cigar box away, and left the shed.

He ran to the wall and looked around. No one was watching. They were all busy trying to organize their little domestic worlds that had fallen apart just a few hours ago. Up Sol went, pulling himself higher and higher on the wooden reinforcements that kept the wall solid and secure.

When he reached the top, he didn't even pause to look back. He jumped, letting his knees give a little to break the force of the fall. And then he ran, his feet digging into the sandy soil, moving as fast as he had ever moved in his life. He knew he'd have to slow soon. But if he could just make it to that grove of trees, he'd be out of sight. Then he could slow down.

Sol flung himself onto the large cottonwood tree, embracing it as if it were an old friend. He caught his breath for a minute, and then took off again, this time at a slower pace.

By the time Sol got to Kohler's place, he figured it was about four o'clock in the afternoon. He was exhausted from running most of the way. He'd probably better rest for a little while and try to find something to eat. It felt strange to go right up to Kohler's house and open the door without knocking. But he knew nobody would be home. The room didn't look much different than before. They hadn't taken much with them. There was the worn old couch. And the picture on the wall.

Sol stopped and studied the picture. Was that Mr. Kohler's father, that frowning man in the black suit? Didn't he hate him after everything he had done? But maybe he loved him, too. Strange how hate and love can share the same space, like salt and pepper share the same table.

There were some carrots in the pantry and some dried apples and beef jerky. This wasn't stealing, was it? If he didn't take the food, the Indians would. And didn't Mr. Kohler owe him something for risking his life to bring in Kohler's horse?

Sol filled his jacket with the food and went out to eat it in Star's stall. What if—by some miracle—Star would *be* there? What if she had made her way back? Carefully Sol opened the barn door and went inside. A sound startled him. Something had moved over by the horses' stalls. Wha . . . ? A hen clucked and flapped her way down from a pile of straw. The stalls were empty.

Sol ate quickly and stuffed the remaining food in his pockets. It might taste pretty good in a few hours. He got a drink from the well and splashed some water onto his face and his arms. It would dry off in a couple of minutes, but right now it felt good.

Sol followed the line of fenceposts. He had dug the holes for most of them himself. He was walking. He didn't have time to walk. Fear, like a large hand at his back, pushed him forward, and he began again to run.

"Please, God," he prayed again, "please let me get to Star before the Indians do." He had been praying for hours now. It was the longest prayer of his life. It went on and on to the beat of his feet on the ground. "Please . . . please . . . please . . . please!"

Sol had walked all day when they crossed the plains in their covered wagon, except for the time when he was sick. But to *run* all day—that was different. No one could run all day. His shirt was wet with sweat, and his feet ached violently. That loud, gasping sound was his breathing.

How did they keep their spirits up over the long miles across the plains? They sang. Maybe it would help now—if he could find the breath.

"With . . . a . . . merry little jig . . . and a . . . gay . . . little . . . song.

Whoa, Haw . . . Buck . . . and Jerry Boy.

We trudge . . . our way . . . the whole . . ."

Sol stopped running and put a hand over his racing heart.

This was crazy. What was he doing? His eyes searched the pastures. No Star. No animals of any kind. Kohler's property didn't end for another couple of miles. He'd have to go on. He'd *have* to.

If he could just find Star, he'd ride her back to Kohler's barn where they could spend the night. The place looked deserted. If the Indians did come through in the night, they probably wouldn't stop. And then the next morning they could race for the fort. *If* he could just find Star. "Please . . . please . . . please. Whoa, Haw, Buck, and . . . Jerry Boy."

The hand of fear pushed again at his back, and even though Sol could run no more, he ran. He stumbled into a little ditch and got up and ran again. His leg stung where he had torn his pants on barbed wire a few hours before.

It was getting dark now. "Please . . . please." His eyes searched the fields desperately. No Star. Sweat and tears mingled on his face.

When it was too dark to run anymore, Sol slowed to a walk. And when it was too dark to walk anymore, he stopped. If Star were in the pastures over there, he wouldn't be able to see her anyway. There were sheep nearby. He could hear them bleating. Maybe there were other animals, too. But he wouldn't be able to see them until dawn. The best thing to do would be to just lie down and try to sleep. And then when it was light, he could go on.

The ground was hard, but it would feel good just to lie down, just to stop moving and rest. Sol felt around with his hands for a grassy spot—that'd be about the best bed he could manage. He took off his jacket and pulled it over him like a small blanket. There were a few dried apples in his pocket, and he chewed on them as he looked up into the night sky. The moon was not full, and the stars were not bright. Sometimes just about all the lights seem to go out, and there's nothing left but darkness.

Sol closed his eyes and continued his prayer. "Please . . . please . . . please."

CHAPTER TEN

W hen Sol next opened his eyes, the lights had gone back on. Morning! Sol jumped to his feet and looked around. There were a dozen or so sheep grazing nearby. But no cattle could be seen. And no horses. No horses at all. Only green, empty fields—and miles of fence posts—and . . .

Smoke? Smoke rising into the pale blue sky from that grove of trees just beyond the creek over there? Someone was here? The white settlers were all in the fort. No one was out here but the . . . Instinctively Sol threw himself onto the ground and pressed his belly against the earth.

Like a snake, he crawled over to a large bush nearby and cautiously raised his head. The creek was about a hundred feet away, and as Sol lay staring at it, two large Indians approached, squat down, put something in the water, and then lifted it out again. Sol put his face into his hands. Last night he had wandered *right into the Ute encampment!* He had slept only a few hundred feet from the Indians!

There was no way out now. Maybe in the dark he could have escaped, but not in broad daylight. The Indians would have their guards posted all over. They always did. If he tried to make a run for it, within minutes there would be an arrow in his back. He knew that.

For minutes he lay pressed against the earth. He was shivering, but not from the cold. The sun felt warm on his back. What would his father do? What would his mother do? Usually Sol prayed on his knees, but he figured God would understand that right now he was safer on his belly.

"Dear Heavenly Father . . ."

Sol had always been taught that it was polite to start a prayer with some "thank you's" instead of just asking for things right off.

". . . Thank you that so far I have not been killed by the Indians. And please help me figure out some way not to get killed at all. Forgive me if it was a stupid thing to come out here, but I had to do it. And please bless Star. And Pa and Ma and Grandma and Eve. And I would really be grateful if I could live a longer time, 'cause I haven't done everything I think I should do. And I'll try to be good . . . if I don't get killed by the Indians. Dear God . . . what should I do . . . ?"

Sol tried to be calm and just listen. And in a moment a voice came into his mind. It sort of sounded like his own voice. But then it also sort of sounded like his mother's voice. And his father's voice.

"Get up," it said. "Walk into the camp. Ask to see Arrowpine."

Sol did not stop to ask questions or to argue. Slowly he got to his knees and then to his feet. Could he be as brave as his mother leading her family out into the yard to confront the dark, staring eyes of the Shoshonis? Could he be as brave as his father riding out alone to see Arrowpine, bearing the chief's dead son and begging him to again talk peace with the white man?

He had his father's sandy hair and his mother's clear blue eyes. Their genes were in his blood. Was their courage there also?

Sol found a stick and put his light blue jacket on it, raising it like a flag. He had nothing white. This would have to do. Then he walked to the creek, through the creek, and up the bank to the other side.

Sol did not hear a sound. And it happened so quickly that he saw nothing. The Indian brave sailed silently through the air and pinned Sol's arms to his sides as the boy and the red man fell to the earth. In an instant Sol's back was pressed to the ground. Wild, black eyes in the painted face above him and a knife held high by the bronze arm made Sol cry out. Was this the end? Was the next breath his last?

"Arrowpine!" said Sol. "I am Arrowpine's friend. Take me to Arrowpine!"

Suddenly a second painted Indian stood beside them, speaking loudly and rapidly in Ute. The brave above Sol grunted and slowly got to his feet. One dark hand grasped Sol's left shoulder and another dark hand grasped his right shoulder. Sol walked between the two Indians toward the camp.

Other red men stopped and stared as they got closer. Sol saw an Indian dash into a teepee. The two at his sides pulled his hands behind him and roughly tied them with rawhide. They didn't need to do that, Sol thought. He could not escape.

The tapping of a drum began. And from everywhere Indians appeared. They stood and stared as Sol was led to a spot by the campfire. The two Indians stood on either side of him, arms folded across their painted chests. The other red men were talking among themselves, gesturing at Sol and, he thought, debating on what his fate should be.

The Indians became silent when Arrowpine emerged from his teepee and walked toward them. Sol lifted his chin high and looked straight at the approaching chief. He would not show any sign of weakness, of fear. He would show him that a white boy was as courageous as an Indian boy.

Arrowpine stopped in front of Sol and looked him directly in the eyes. Sol did not blink. His mouth felt too dry even to open, but Sol managed to part his lips and speak.

"Hello, Arrowpine," he said.

Arrowpine narrowed his eyes and continued to stare at him. Did he recognize him? It had been a year since he had seen the chief, and everyone was always telling Sol how much he was changing, how much like a man he was looking. For once Sol was not glad.

"You know me, Chief." Sol attempted to smile. The muscles of his face could barely be moved, but Sol tried. "I'm Sol McAllister—John Mac's boy. John Mac good friend to Arrowpine."

The Indian who had gone to find Arrowpine began to speak rapidly in Ute. His hands gestured wildly and his voice was high and hard.

Arrowpine listened a moment, still looking at Sol, and then spoke. "He say, 'Kill white boy. Great Spirit has sent white boy to go to Indian hunting ground with Arrowpine son.'"

"No, Chief!" Sol tried to take a step toward Arrowpine, but was restrained by the hands of his Indian guards. "Great Spirit does not want that. He does not want killing. He wants *nobody* killed. Great Spirit wants you to let me go back to my people. He wants the Indian and the white man to live in peace."

The brave beside Arrowpine spoke again in the Indian tongue, rapid, violent words as sharp as tomahawks. Then he drew a knife from his belt and lifted it above his head with both hands, holding it there, waiting for Arrowpine's permission to strike.

"No!" cried Sol. "I am Arrowpine's friend." Sol thrust his head to one side so the necklace could be seen. "Look . . . here is the necklace you gave me. I helped save you from the Shoshonis. I brought you to your camp. I am Arrowpine's friend."

The Indian with the knife cried out in impatience and shook the weapon above his head.

Arrowpine studied the boy for a moment, a moment that was longer than any moment Sol had ever known. And then he turned to the brave beside him, raised his hand, and took the knife.

Sol did not breathe. Did Arrowpine want to do the job himself? Would he raise the knife and plunge it into Sol's heart in payment for the death of his own son?

Arrowpine looked at the knife in his hands, looked into the clear blue eyes of the white boy in front of him, and then he tossed the knife into the dust.

The brave shrieked, said something in Ute, lunged for his knife, and walked away in disgust.

Sol felt his knees weaken, and then a surge of strength move through him, all in an instant.

"White boy save Arrowpine from Shoshonis. Arrowpine save white boy from Utes. Go back to your people."

The two Indians untied the rawhide, and Sol's arms fell free. He was about to say thank you and then turn and go. But there was a voice speaking in his head, that same voice. Was it his? His father's? His mother's? "Ask Arrowpine to come to the pow-wow," it said.

Arrowpine had turned and was about to go back to his teepee when Sol spoke. "Chief Arrowpine," he said.

The chief turned and looked at him in surprise.

"Chief . . . you must come to the pow-wow. All other chiefs will be there, but without the Ute tribe represented— without *you* there—treaty of peace will mean nothing. Please come!"

Arrowpine took a step toward Sol and folded his arms. Pain moved across his face as he spoke. "No talk peace with white man. Arrowpine no trust white man. White man lie, kill. White man promise and break promise. White man speak with forked tongue. Arrowpine no talk peace with white man."

Sol closed his eyes and lowered his head. Arrowpine would not come. War between the Utes and the settlers would go on and on. It wasn't fair! It wasn't right!

The sound of running horses was heard. Sol opened his eyes and turned to see a small herd of horses coming into the encampment. Indians yipped and drove the horses through the clearing. White men's horses. His father's horses! He knew them immediately!

Sol felt anger rise within him. He knew he was in no position to criticize. A moment ago he had almost been killed. But the injustice of it all swelled and rolled within him, and he found himself shouting.

"Those aren't your horses! You have no right to steal them! If you steal and kill just because some white men lie and some white men kill, you're no better than they are!"

Arrowpine was looking at Sol with hard, dark eyes.

"Those are my father's horses! He never stole from you . . . never lied to you . . . never killed an Indian. He's risked his life to help the Indians. He prays to the Great Spirit for peace with the Indians. And then you go and steal his horses. It's not fair!"

Tears were in Sol's eyes, but he swallowed and stared them away. He would not let the Indians see him cry.

The hard face of the chief softened, and he took a step toward Sol. "John Mac friend to Arrowpine. John Mac only honest white man of all white men. Arrowpine not take John Mac horses."

Arrowpine spoke in Ute to several of his braves, who quickly went over to the large herd into which Sol's father's horses had been driven. In a moment the entire herd was moving, slowly coming toward Sol and Arrowpine.

"You show me which horses are your horses. You take them with you. But only yours." Arrowpine motioned his braves to lead the horses in front of Sol.

There was the big brown stallion his father liked to ride. "That one is ours!" Sol pointed. And there was the pinto mare they'd bought last spring. "That one is ours!"

The braves led out from the others the horses Sol indicated. "And that one . . . and that one." Sol's heart warmed, and he felt himself smiling. He could ride up to the fort with his father's horses! "That one is ours . . . and that one." There. All six horses that had been left behind. His father and mother would be so . . .

Suddenly another horse left the herd and trotted over to Sol, whinnying in excitement. Star! There was Star, nuzzling her nose into Sol's neck. Sol put his arms around her and pressed his cheek into hers.

"Hi, Star," he whispered. "Oh, hi!"

"This horse yours?" demanded Arrowpine.

Sol jerked back and looked into Star's warm, dark eyes. He couldn't breathe. He couldn't think.

Arrowpine's voice came again. "This your horse?"

Sol opened his mouth to speak. Why not say yes? The Indian chief would never know. He could save Star! He could save her from being traded to another tribe or driven to California where he'd never see her again! The filly's breath was warm on Sol's neck. Why not say yes?

But then something quick and cold, like a sudden shower in spring, began at the roots of Sol's hair and moved down, down through every part of his body, down through his blood and over his skin. The voice was clear in his mind—the voice that sounded like his and also sounded like . . .

"No." Sol could barely hear the word as he spoke it. "No. This horse is not mine." Sol closed his eyes and turned his face away from Star's. "She belongs to Nat Kohler." Tears were coursing down Sol's cheeks, and he made no effort to hide them.

"I know," said Arrowpine.

Sol slowly turned to the chief. Through the blur of his tears, he saw Arrowpine looking at him with a strange expression on his face.

"You know?" asked Sol.

Arrowpine pointed to Kohler's brand on Star's black hide. "See? No bar-M. I know horse not yours."

The Indian chief was silent for a moment, and then spoke again. "Go. Go back to people."

Sol put a hand on Star's cheek and looked deep into her eyes. "Goodbye, Star. Goodbye."

Then Sol climbed onto the big brown stallion and drove the other five horses in front of him. He looked back at the Indians who were watching him go, back at Star, back at the herd of stolen horses, and back at Chief Arrowpine who was untying his own horse from in front of his teepee, mounting it, and riding toward Sol.

When Arrowpine's horse was abreast of Sol's, the chief looked over at the white boy and spoke. "We go."

Sol looked at him questioningly. We go? Arrowpine was coming, too?

"Arrowpine meet with white man. Pow-wow. Talk for peace. If *one* white boy honest . . . maybe . . ." The wrinkles of Arrowpine's face softened, and his dark eyes looked far off into the distance. "Maybe . . . are more."

The Indian chief shouted back at his braves, and in a moment the herd of horses — *all* the horses — began to move.

They galloped in silence, Arrowpine, the white boy, a dozen or so Indian braves, and more than a hundred white man's horses.

Sol rode high on the big brown stallion, higher than he had ever ridden in his life. Arrowpine was coming to talk peace! The horses would be returned to their owners! The wind moved across Sol's skin and through his hair. A smile was on his face, set as if on clay that had been sunned into a permanent form. He rode and smiled and rode and smiled.

When they approached the fort, they slowed their pace. Sol knew that if they could see the fort, the guards in the towers could see them.

"Let me ride ahead," Sol said to Arrowpine. "You come behind me."

Arrowpine took from a pouch a white flag and lifted it on his bow. Then he signaled Sol to lead out and followed perhaps thirty feet behind him. Directly back of him rode six braves on their prancing ponies, and behind them moved the herd of horses, a number of Indian braves bringing up the rear.

Sol led the strange parade, still smiling. He knew what was

happening in the fort. The guards had alerted the settlers that Indians were approaching. And then one of them had said something like, "Why, look . . . that's a white boy. Why . . . why that's . . . Sol McAllister!" And then John and Paula and Grandma would come running. They were probably peering out of the rifle holes right now, wondering what in tarnation Sol was doing out there with the Indians. They'd be glad to see him. He knew that. But would they be afraid?

Sol reined in his horse about a hundred feet from the fort. His eyes scoured the towers and the walls for any sign of life. There was none.

"Pa?" he shouted. "Pa?"

After a moment his father's voice was heard, choked with emotion. "Are you all right, son?"

"I'm fine, Pa. I've brought Arrowpine. He wants to talk peace. He'll go to the pow-wow. And he's giving back all the white man's horses. Will you come out and talk to him, Pa?"

"Tell him bring Nat Kohler," said Arrowpine, who had ridden up near to Sol. "Kohler and Arrowpine pow-wow."

"And bring Mr. Kohler with you, Pa," Sol shouted. "Arrowpine wants to talk with him. He'll be safe. Bring guards if you want."

Sol and Arrowpine sat on their horses, white flag waving in the breeze, while the large door of the fort slowly creaked open. A dozen men with rifles in their hands came out first. Then John McAllister. And then Nat Kohler, walking slowly, slowly, as slowly as Sol had ever seen anybody walk. The men with rifles stayed near the fort while John and Kohler walked toward Sol and Arrowpine.

John raised his arm in greeting as he arrived at the two horses. "Hello, Chief . . . son." John looked like a man who had not slept all night.

"I'm sorry, Pa," said Sol. "I know you were worried—but I *had* to!"

"It's all right, son. I would have been out hunting for you . . . but I knew, I just *knew* that you were all right."

Funny what you can know, thought Sol. If you'll just listen.

Arrowpine handed the white flag to Sol and put away his bow. Then he looked directly at Nat Kohler, who was staring at the ground as if an interesting story were written there.

"You kill Arrowpine son!"

Kohler looked up at the Indian chief, his eyes filled with guilt and fear. He said nothing.

"You kill Arrowpine son," the chief said again, pointing a long brown finger at the trembling white man. "I planned to take your life. But I have decided to make peace with white man. So I take your horse instead. That one!" He turned and pointed to Star who was grazing with the other horses on the few patches of grass available. "Need horse," Arrowpine went on, "for present for my friend, Sol."

Kohler stared at the chief, and his thick mouth fell open. "My . . . my horse? Shore, Chief. Why, shore! Whatever you say, Chief!"

Sol stared at the chief, too, and his mouth fell open. But no words came.

"Sol Mac good friend to Arrowpine. He good, brave, honest boy. He have horse . . . present from Arrowpine!"

The Indian chief was smiling. Sol had never seen him smile before. He looked different when he smiled. When people smile, they all look sort of the same.

Slowly Sol slid from the back of the big brown stallion. Slowly he turned to Star. And then he let out a whoop, a whoop loud enough to startle both the white men with the rifles and the red men with the horses. Then he ran. He ran like there were Indians behind him. Which there were, but they were mostly smiling and even laughing.

Sol threw himself onto Star's neck. "Did you hear that, Star? You're mine! You're mine!" Then he jumped onto the filly's back and without saddle, without bridle, raced off into the fields. His hands held the filly's mane, and his knees gently urged her on. He couldn't help himself. He called out to the

Indians, to the horses, to the fort, to his father, to Kohler, to the sky, "She's mine! She's mine!"

"He . . . uh . . . he likes the horse," said Nat Kohler, and his grin was almost a real smile.

"He *loves* the horse," corrected John.

More than anything else, Sol's father wanted a lasting peace with the Indians. And more than anything else, Sol wanted a horse of his own. Remarkable that they both came on the same day and in the same way.

"We'll just go to that grove of trees and then back to the fort, okay?" Sol put his head close to Star's ear as he talked to her.

Boy and horse raced over the field. He didn't want to tire her out on their first run. Pretty soon he'd take her into the fort and give her a bag of oats and a good brushing. And some water. After all, if Sol were a horse, that's what he would like someone to do unto him.